MW00573872

PRAISE FOR *REIMAGINE TEAMS*

"Mark Samuel's new book, *Reimagine Teams*, is one of the most useful and inspirational works I've read on a subject of crucial importance: team building. As I've told three generations of clients, 'Great teams build great businesses.' There is no better place to look for the secrets of great team-building than this book."
— Gay Hendricks, Ph.D., President of the Hendricks Institute and Best-Selling Author of *The Big Leap*

"No one combines the human warmth of compassionate, conscious business leadership with cold-blooded commitment to bottom-line results like Mark Samuel. This book, *Reimagine Teams*, is his most powerful yet, and it puts him in his rightful place at the very top of the world's most effective leadership mentors."
— Steve Chandler, Best-Selling Author of *Time Warrior*

"*Reimagine Teams* is a road map for implementing Mark's Breakthrough B STATE model and was very impactful within our hospital. The precision of developing 'Team Habits for Collective Execution' created a high level of cross-functional team performance that yielded significant improvements in financial, quality, and human resource outcomes."
— Susan Juris, Retired President of UH Ahuja Medical Center

"*Reimagine Teams* inspired me to turn my way of thinking about team dynamics upside down. With Mark Samuel's captivating examples and powerful framework, we now have a way to approach team improvement that leads to lasting and significant change. This book will save leaders countless hours of frustration focusing on symptoms instead of the root causes of team breakdowns."
— Jamie Woolf, Director of Culture and Learning at Pixar Animation Studios (Pixar)

"Too many leaders think relationship building is all that's needed for an effective cross-functional team. Mark delivers a simple and insightful leadership model for what it really takes to become a cross-functional team."
— Shawn Slusser, Vice President of Sales and Marketing at Infineon Technologies North America, Inc.

"Mark Samuel has revealed how, as leaders, we have been using wrong strategies to make people work together. By focusing on building trust, we have not only been reactive, but we have also been misdiagnosing the root causes of dysfunctional teams. I believe the clarifying ENDS, MEANS, COORDINATION, and RELATIONSHIPS model is key to building high-performing teams and I plan to add it in my toolbox. *Reimagine Teams* is a must for a leader at any level."
— Misheck Mwaba, Ph.D., President and CEO of Bow Valley College in Calgary, Canada

"The case study presentation style of *Reimagine Teams* allowed me to immediately relate and identify the applicability of this fresh approach to my own team. Mark Samuel has done a great job of presenting his unique approach to staying ahead of relationship issues and achieving the end goal. This book will be a benefit to any leader working to focus their team on a common goal."
— Bob Franssen, Site Vice President at Grand Gulf Nuclear Station

"*Reimagine Teams* is critically important in today's business environment. Mark's practical approach to building teams that focus on 'collective execution' to optimize coordination is essential for people geographically spread and blended between the office and virtual space. Without building cross-functional 'team habits,' organizations would be left to operate in silos undermining future success."
— Stephen Chenard, Vice President of Supply Chain Integration at General Dynamics Mission Systems

"*Reimagine Teams* helped me understand the essential connection between where we want to go as a business and the way we work together on a day-to-day basis to get there. Both are key elements to make sure that as a team we are walking together through a growth and sustainable path. I recommend this book to every business leader that wishes to achieve breakthrough results in a consistent way."
— Lorenzo Garavito, CEO of Iris Bank, Colombia

"*Reimagine Teams* makes you question your education, your MBA, and every consultant you've worked with before. Only by under-standing the concepts in this book will you be able to achieve sustained execution and results by having the courage to depend on aligned colleagues working together for success."
— Elaine Vincent, Chief Administrative Officer for the Town of Okotoks, Canada

"As a commercial manager, I used Mark's team-building strategy described in *Reimagine Teams* to move a nationwide sales team to work together to achieve corporate goals. Our Team Habits that drove our Team Outcomes produced fantastic results for our company and our Team Relationships were never better. I plan to use *Reimagine Teams* as a strategy to lead my current company."
— Carlos Echeverri, CEO of Merkaorgánico, Colombia

"In *Reimagine Teams*, Mark Samuel disrupts old ways of thinking about building high-performing teams and hands you a masterful and practical new way of approaching one of the most important things we do in business—working together to achieve outcomes. The focus on 'execution-based' trust is a game changer for rapidly and boldly creating a high-performance team."
— Alison Greer, Director of People Strategy at MagicLinks

PRAISE FOR MARK SAMUEL'S PREVIOUS WORK

"I played for one remarkable team and for one great city almost all of my baseball career. Mark Samuel supports what I have always believed: The commitments we make and keep to ourselves and the people in our lives are the key to achieving our genuine dreams."
— Ernie Banks, "Mr. Cub" Baseball Hall of Famer, 512 career homerun-hitter

"*Making Yourself Indispensable: The Power of Personal Accountability* is an inspiring guide to being accountable in all aspects of your life—from work to home to relationships ... a road map to achievement and a source of practical wisdom."
— Arianna Huffington, Founder of the *Huffington Post* and Thrive Global

"An inspirational and practical guide for self-improvement. I recommend it to anyone who wants to become the CEO of their own life."
— Ken Blanchard, Best-Selling Co-Author of *The One Minute Manager* and *Leadership Pill*

"Mark Samuel has created a new paradigm in thinking about how to address the major challenges facing business today. He provides a step-by-step road map for companies to move from an 'A State' culture to a (Breakthrough) B STATE culture ... for building a world-class organization."
— Al Cornish, System Vice President of Learning and Organizational Development and Chief Learning Officer at Norton Healthcare

"Mark Samuel takes accountability to higher breakthrough levels and is a must-read for all leaders at any level of the organization … I plan on using his many golden nuggets in my professional and personal life."

— Fadi Diya, Senior Vice President and Chief Nuclear Officer at Ameren Corporation

"I have focused on business and organizational transformation for the last twenty-five years and I can attest that the key levers that Mark describes in this book actually do work: powerful shared purpose, collaborative vs. siloed priorities, a forward focus on building positive energy, and scale vs. dwelling on the problem—these are pillars of successful transformation."

— Victor Cho, CEO of Evite

"We transformed our organization to a new (Breakthrough) B STATE, and it is like being a new organization. This book can transform your organization and your personal life very quickly."

— Ron Peterson, President and CEO of Baxter Regional Medical Center

"Mark Samuel is a proven expert on leadership and break-through results. His knowledge of the workplace, its challenges, and the tools to overcome those challenges leads to a powerful and significant read for all business owners, managers, and supervisors. His road map for success breaks down silo behavior, produces excellent teamwork throughout the organization, and truly drives outcomes and results."

— Frank Dulcich, CEO and President of Pacific Seafood Group

"Mark Samuel proposes a simple, revolutionary mindset shift and an approach that is life-changing for all leaders, managers, and the companies they work for on all levels, professionally and personally."

— Rúna Bouius, Transformational Leadership Expert, Speaker, and Author

"He's done it again! Mark Samuel has written another compelling, relevant, and engaging book ... with practical tips, and critical insight to help leaders drive organizational performance to meet desired outcomes and goals."
— Jim Barnes, CEO of enVista

"This book provides abundant, practical, and savvy advice for leaders and individual contributors alike, on how to move with confidence toward desired outcomes."
— Gene Gerrard, Vice President of Human Resources for TOTE, Inc.

"Mark Samuel provides a paradigm shift to quickly transform your business and culture by changing your 'habits of collective execution.' This is not only a refreshing approach that gets measurable results, but also a must-read for executives and leaders."
— Joey Hubbard, Global Head of Training at Thrive Global

"Mark Samuel reveals a truly breakthrough way of leaving behind the endless loops of frustration that I call Conscious Business."
— Russell Bishop, Author of *Workarounds That Work* and CEO of Conscious Living

"Mark uses authentic and tangible examples—like stories about drumming and baseball, and how these relate to business ... he addresses how we work together, our attitudes, and actions are the key to our transformation."
— Darwin Richardson, Senior Vice President of Quality and Regulatory Affairs at BPL Plasma

"The principles and practices expressed provide a clear, concise pathway for easy and efficient application in today's competitive business environment."
— Cindy Tucker, America's Senior Customer Contact and Business Center Manager for Agilent Technologies

REIMAGINE
TEAMS

The Missing Piece in Team Building to
Achieve Breakthrough Results

REIMAGINE
TEAMS

The Missing Piece in Team Building to
Achieve Breakthrough Results

Mark Samuel
with Sarah Samuel

Published by Best Seller Publishing®, St. Augustine, FL
Best Seller Publishing® is a registered trademark.
Printed in the United States of America.
ISBN:978-1-956649-18-5

For more information, please write:
Best Seller Publishing®
53 Marine Street
St. Augustine, FL 32084
or call 1 (626) 765-9750
Visit us online at: www.BestSellerPublishing.org

TABLE OF CONTENTS

ACKNOWLEDGMENTS

As I look back over my life, it has been all about teams.

It takes a team of people to write a book. There are two people most important to me and to the process of writing this book. I am so grateful for their loving support, incredible demonstration of excellence, and unwavering encouragement.

Sarah Samuel—my daughter and, more importantly, an amazingly creative and gifted writer and brilliant thinker who assisted me throughout the process of writing *Reimagine Teams* and helped to expand my consciousness about diversity.

Kamin Samuel—my beautiful wife and true love, who is my constant inspiration for believing in myself, my role model for loving accountability, and an example for keeping my focus on gratitude and service.

BSP Publishing Team & The OC Recording Company

The team at BSP led me through the process with writing, publishing, and marketing *Reimagine Teams* worldwide. Thanks for your professionalism, support, and commitment to excellence.

Rob Kosberg, Bob Harpole, Matthew Schnarr, Burke Mohan, Anna Rowser, Lizze Slocum, Kathleen Shewman, May Cheng, and Meghan McDonald.

Asaf Fulks was a great partner in recording the audiobook.

Family—Our Most Valuable Team

Our most valuable team in our lives is our family if relationships are based on loving, respect, forgiveness, and honoring each person's unique gifts. My family includes relatives and friends who are my loving mentors and teammates in the game of life.

Mike Samuel and Meta Samuel (in memoriam), loving parents who wanted the best for me and taught me teamwork from the time I was nine years old.

Nancy Grossman-Samuel—dedicated and loving mother to Sarah Samuel, continual loving support, and best friend.

Laurie Grossman-Wright and Jane Grossman—aunts to Sarah Samuel, continual loving support, and wonderfully loving family members.

Sophie Chiche—loving mother to Léah and Charles Miller and stepmother to Sarah Samuel, continual loving support, and best friend.

Léah Miller—loving, creative, and generous stepchild who reminds me to appreciate art and helped to expand my consciousness about diversity.

Martine Chiche and Laurent Chiche—grandparent and uncle to Léah Miller and loving supporters and family members.

Danny Miller—father to Léah and Charlie Miller, loving friend, amazing writer, and awesome model of fatherhood.

Robert (in memoriam) and Dr. Marion Bell—loving parents to Kamin and wonderful educators and role models for family, community, and church leadership.

Kelvin, Kristie, Keane Bell—siblings to Kamin and loving, talented, and accomplished leaders who generously take care of one another, their children, and their parents.

My closest cousins, best friends, and awesome mentors and role models for family, community, and business leadership.

Sandi, Paul, Adam, and Mitch Caplan, Barbara State (in memoriam), Hannah State, Robin State Yaakov, and Sylvia Novack (in memoriam)—Mel Gunn, Davee Gunn, and Virginia Bert—Ruth and Art Penn, Faye, Sharon, Rhonda, and Allan Penn—Barry and Fern Krugel, Carol Krugel Ellstein, Melissa Fellman—Merle Levine, Marvin (in memoriam) and Reinette Levine, and Michael Levine.

Friends who are family and mentors who have all guided me on my path and whose loving lasts the tests of time.

Laura Hillman (in memoriam), Robert and Margot Hillman, Polly Clitheroe (in memoriam), Chip and Kerry Clitheroe, Elaine Heiser (in memoriam), Mike and Linda Heiser, David and Teresa Rodgers, Licia and David Rester, Todd and Tamara Alexander, Hal Brand, Kevin Brand, Thomas Hempelmann, Annie Hyman Pratt, Barbara Schindler, Heather McGonigal, JD Bowles, Sue and Ken Bingham, Paul and Cindy Henry, Sinan and Kai Kanatsiz, Kevin Maloney, Izzy Ellerby, Jonathan and Yousha Ellerby, Charlie and Pam Hedges, Agapi Stassinopoulos, Arianna Huffington, Marc and Tanya Fields, Mark and Grace Hennings, Kevin Lamp, Alcene and Bob Looper, Kent and Linda Falk, Phyllis Mitz, Tom Boyer, Paul Riley, Geri Lopker, Leslie Boyer, Jason Gulinare, Greg Nichols and Jennifer Love, Annette Shaked, Darwin Richardson, Thomas Vehec, Dale Atkinson, Fadi Diya, Ira Needleman, Kathrene Hansen, Kathy LaMarr-Bines, Liz Schulz, Gene Gerrard and Lynn Takaki, Frank Dulcich, Paul and Lois Vallerga, and Candy Spitzer, Kevin McMillan, Barbara Thrasher, Kristen Cumming, Mark Frezell, Fiona Coffey, Carrie Doubts, Sashua Benay, Michelle Scott, Malika Lee, Donna Bond, Berti Klein, Alexandra Diez Barroso—all whose friendship is as loving as any family member along with being mentors in business and role models for unconditional loving.

IMPAQ—B STATE Team

The IMPAQ—B STATE Team have all been visionaries, mentors, and loving supporters for my growth and paradigm-shifting ideas that they helped create and put into practice. There are so many more people to acknowledge who have traveled in and out of IMPAQ over the years, so I am only focusing on those who are present and who have become part of my family.

David Rodgers, DSS—Executive Leader within IMPAQ and loving business partner who continually demonstrates excellence, learning, and leadership for his clients and within IMPAQ.

Jane Grossman—Master Trainer and Consultant who has led our biggest projects and operates with the highest levels of integrity, loving and caring for her clients.

Anthony Escamilla—Director of Operations who provides humor, direct feedback, and dedicated service to clients and consultants alike.

Sarah Wilson—Master Public Relations and Social Media Expert who has been creatively getting the message out on the power of B STATE Transformation.

Scott Wilson (twiz.io)—SEO Optimization Expert who has been a great support in messaging our unique methodology so that others can engage with us directly.

Other team members, associates, and colleagues include Sarah Samuel, Marianne Kruse, Lei Lani Fera, Allan Matos, Susan Juris, Steve Dickey, Jeff Freedman, Laurel Taylor, Sharon Rich, Heather Ridenoure, Ruth Coleman, Annika Laale, Stefanie Fenton, Scott Span, Stacia Topping, Barri Harris, Laszlo A. Retfalvi, and Nate Johnson.

Coaching Group and Associates in Latin America

Eduardo Elleras, Marcela Valencia, Ana Cecilia Ginge, Fernando (Nano) Escallón, Luis Manuel Ramirez, and Natalia Liévano

Rainmen and Associates in Europe

Marcos Cajina, Robert Nieuwland, Catherine Clercx, Jaco Jansen, Robbert van Waart, Geert Stradmeijer, Frank Brilman, Marco Scheele, and Edo Noppert

RelatUcation powered by BFSD Global in Australia and Asia-Pacific

Valerie Lew-Kiedrowski

Sports Coaches and Mentors

There are many baseball and basketball coaches who taught me the values, honor, and dedication of being part of high-performance teams—promoting individual excellence AND teamwork. Many believed in me when I didn't believe in myself and guided me in life, learning healthy competition and supportive teamwork: Jay Green, Bill Chapman, Sr. (in memoriam), Mr. Clampett (in memoriam), Walter Lamp, Sr. (in memoriam), Mike Lamp, Dennis Lamp, Jim Rodarte (in memoriam), Dave Hernandez (in memoriam), and Wendel Witt (in memoriam).

Music Conductors and Musicians

Music is about listening, adapting, and loving what you do. These conductors and musicians guided me, helped me to grow up, and supported me in the most loving ways:

Dr. Michael Pappone, Scott Avery, Keith Hedges, Don Wigton, Ron Lira, Steve Montague, Steve Liss, John Knopf, Al Fogle, Kim Lenz, Mahan Jiwan Kaur Khalsa, Rick Palomo, Eric Lumiere, James and Karen Gilbert Hassett, Jesus Garcia, John Morgan, Gabe Morgan, Joshua Hayes, Peter Hastings, and Allie Willis (in memoriam).

Educators and Consultants Who Demonstrated Individual Excellence within Team Settings

There are those special educators and mentors throughout life who light the way for self-loving, respect, personal accountability, and teamwork. These educators all represent mentors in my life who helped to shape me into understanding the true values of teamwork and individual self-expression: Mrs. Reidy (sixth grade teacher), Alcene Holzman, Dr. Marty (Charlie) Brotman (in memoriam), Robert Newcomb, Ph.D. (in memoriam), Newton Marguillies, Ph.D., Cheryl Malakoff, Tracy Quinton, Gene Thin Elk, David Covey, Stephan Mardyks, Michael Nila, Joerg Schmitz, Merv Donner, John Rothmann, John-Roger, DSS, John Morton, DSS and Leigh Taylor-Young Morton, Drs. Ron and Mary Hulnick, Paul Kaye, DSS, Vincent Dupont, DSS, Mark Lurie, DSS, Michael and Alicia Hayes, Lawrence and Janet Caminite, Stu and Candace Semigran, David Bransky, Joey Hubbard, DSS, David and Kathryn Allen, Russell Bishop, Sally McGhee, Dr. Gregory Stebbins, and Jennifer Cayer, and Steve Chandler, Devon Bandison, Vicki Guy, and Drs. Gay and Katie Hendricks.

I have been blessed with amazing family, friends, coaches, mentors, and educators who contributed to my growth and transformation—many more than I can even list in this book. Thank you for your generosity of spirit and love!

INTRODUCTION

TEAMS ARE THE HEART OF ORGANIZATIONS

"We have to go for what we think we're fully capable of, not
limit ourselves by what we've been in the past."

—Vivek Paul

After writing five books on the topics of personal accountability, organizational accountability, and rapidly implementing change to achieve breakthrough results, I am finally coming full circle to my roots and writing a book on building high-performing teams. The current models for building teams haven't changed in over forty years, and the effectiveness of those methods is questionable at best. I learned this the hard way as a young team-building consultant. I was getting great reviews but subpar results. While my clients were learning a lot about building trust in relationships, communicating better, and resolving conflict, they weren't actually working better as a team. Their execution was still poor, and the business results and culture change they were looking for were still elusive, at least long-term.

This put me on a thirty-five-year journey of refining my techniques and developing a program that not only improves interpersonal relationships between team members but actually improves teamwork execution and business outcomes as a result, sustaining the organization for more than a decade. I used my background in statistics to start measuring team effectiveness—not just relationships and how people *feel* on the team but the results they produce and their effectiveness in producing those results. Based on measurable correlations between results, performance, and relationships, we discovered the "missing piece" that team-building methodologies aren't including.

In thirty-five years, I've worked with over 30,000 team members in 1,400 teams spanning twenty countries to introduce the missing piece. Over 97.5% have achieved measurable breakthrough results that they were not able to get with traditional team building.

Unfortunately, team building and change management practices haven't changed with me; the gold standard for building teams is still the archaic idea of focusing on relationships, which are often the symptom, rather than the source, of team breakdown.

This book will teach you about the missing piece that I discovered and have used with all of my clients to create consistent, *measurable* results. You'll learn a new mindset, approach, practical steps, and the tools necessary to develop different kinds of teams with effective and sustainable team building. All the stories in this book are true, though I've changed or omitted names of both people and organizations to protect their privacy. Everything I share is based on personal experience and practice rather than academic philosophy, which I've found doesn't always translate successfully into practice.

I wrote this book for any team leader, team facilitator, C-level executive, or external consultant or coach who works with teams to improve their functioning, output, and results. If you are, like I was, tired of using team-building books and best practices only to experience inconsistent results, slow change, and a lack of sustainable results, this book is for you.

You will learn about Collective Execution and Team Habits that change the game for building teams—the way top-performing athletic teams, music groups, and business teams do to create stellar results. You will read stories from teams at all levels from different industries and different-sized organizations that have accomplished breakthrough results within three to twelve months and sustained them for multiple years.

By reading this book, you will learn the following strategies:

- Changing the culture of a team within two days, as demonstrated by a new mindset and behaviors for working together to drive business results
- Applying a new approach to team meetings that focuses more on resolving problems, breakdowns, and conflicts than sharing information or hearing updates
- Establishing "Shared Ownership" and cross-functional accountability to eliminate silo thinking and behavior
- Instead of having to move through the phases of Storming, Forming, Norming, and Performing before getting results, move right to Norming and Performing first
- Establishing meaningful measurements that not only assess Team Relationships but also include Team Outcomes and Team Habits
- Getting the full picture of a team for "root cause" analysis to resolve breakdowns, rather than assuming it's a relationship issue
- Learning a process for building teams at any level that evolves as the team changes, improves, or must transform as the business evolves

I invite you to not only gain new insights from this book but also to try out these ideas and learn from your own experience.

I applaud you in taking the plunge and look forward to hearing about your successes!

For the visual learners, I've gathered a few videos so that you can see me present the models in Chapters 4, 5, and 8. You can find resources for this book at bstate.com/rt-resources.

You'll also find an exclusive assessment to gauge the current effectiveness of your team. You may want to take that assessment before reading the book so that you'll know what to pay extra attention to as you read *Reimagine Teams*.

1

HOW I LEARNED A
PIECE WAS MISSING

"Man cannot discover new oceans unless he has the courage
to lose sight of the shore."

—André Gide

FORMAL EDUCATION—1976 TO 1983

My parents taught me to respect authority, and to them that meant not
challenging or questioning my teachers. Whatever my teachers taught me
was already "proven" to be successful, and they were definitely smarter
than me. Whether I had a great teacher or a bad teacher, I was never to
question what I was taught.

At the University of California, Irvine, it was no different, especially
in regard to a professor like Dr. Newton Margulies—Newt, as he called
himself—a fun, joyful, inspiring professor who was also a famous author
in the field of Organizational Development and the first professor I had
who also worked in the field he taught. He was also an external consultant
who led major change efforts using team-building programs for TRW,
the Transportation Department (CalTrans), and many other businesses in
Southern California.

Newt was revered by professors and students alike. I got the privilege of learning from Newt in 1976 when I was just beginning my graduate studies in marketing at UC Irvine. After studying with him, I quickly changed my focus from Marketing to Organizational Development, and Newt became my mentor throughout my time at Irvine and for three years after I graduated. He was the first published author I had met, was credible as a consultant, and his colleagues were Organizational Development legends. In fact, he even had Dr. Peter Drucker speak to our class! He didn't just teach us theory, he gave us the tools and methodology to build teams, which combined practical human psychology with organizational dynamics that had a proven track record of success.

Having the opportunity to learn from these internationally recognized OD gurus, it was natural that I believed what I was taught without question and didn't even think to consider my own experience participating in teams, which I had done since I was nine years old.

I learned all of the best practices in what I refer to now as typical business team building. Typical business team building hasn't changed much since the 1980s when I first learned it and generally consists of some mix of the following:

Team-Building Games

Games used for building team awareness include building bicycles, desert survival exercises, and puzzles. Each one has a different purpose but involves supporting team members in understanding the importance of teams and team behaviors. While this can be a fun awareness and experience for team members, it doesn't translate to clear expectations of how to optimize team execution back in the workplace.

Style Inventories

There are many kinds of style assessments, including the Myers-Briggs test, the DiSC profile, and the Enneagram. These are positive tools for improving understanding of different approaches to communicating and gaining empathy for diverse perspectives. However, it reinforces the emphasis on the individual, rather than being outcome driven, which is the basis for optimizing Collective Execution. Can you imagine a sports team that worked out their plays based on the individual preferences of each team member?

Creating Team Guidelines

Creating team guidelines can be helpful at the beginning of a team-building session to develop a safe approach for people to communicate with one another, demonstrating respect and open listening. But when team members agree to the guidelines, there's often no intention or account-ability for actually keeping the guideline. Of course, when anyone's humanness shows up and they do break the guideline, it often becomes the excuse for not trusting the team member or the entire team-building experience.

Conflict Management Skills

The ability to effectively have difficult conversations and address conflicts is an important skill, but it is largely reactive. The purpose of effective team building is to minimize the number of unnecessary conflicts or diffi-cult conversations. It's about creating the environment for open discussion and disagreement with a customized process for making aligned decisions that reflect the team's unique situation and desired outcomes.

Team Visions

It can be a very motivating process to gain alignment on a general team vision statement that represents the team. These can typically take between a half-day and several days to complete. The problem is that many vision statements become platitudes that sound good but don't have much substance, causing people to feel it was a useless waste of time six months later. Additionally, there's no way to measure your progress to achieving it a year later, so it isn't very useful to the team.

Action Planning

This process is very helpful in transforming the learning from the team-building session into action plans that team members commit to taking after the team-building experience. But once team members get back to their normal work activity, the set of actions they committed to becomes overwhelming and less of a priority. Without follow-through on the team-building commitments, the team loses trust in their team experience and reverts to individual silo behavior.

Since the 1960s, Organizational Development experts have believed that building relationships using the above activities and processes is the best and most effective way to build teams, and this is what I learned while earning my Master's Degree in Business and Organization Development at UC Irvine.

My education proved effective as I implemented several team-building programs after graduating that provided the highest scores possible in client satisfaction. After five successful years, I was shocked to discover that even implementing the best team-building practices known at that time and receiving top mark evaluations weren't giving me the results I wanted—something was missing!

THE SHOCKING FAILURE THAT LED ME TO REEVALUATE THE "EXPERTS"

In 1983, I facilitated a team-building session for a leadership team that had many issues. Their trust, support, and respect for one another were very low, and they weren't on the same page about the direction of the organization; some wanted to make changes, while others wanted to keep the status quo. They didn't respect decisions made by the team and implemented only what was good for their own department. Their communication to the rest of the organization gave conflicting messages, often telling their direct reports things like, "The team decided on this change, but I didn't agree, so just go through the motions to make it look like you are implementing the decision until it gets reversed."

After the team-building effort, everyone was excited about the results. During the program, we developed Team Agreements, resolved conflicts between team members, and developed a vision that everyone was aligned with and enthusiastic about implementing. They learned about each other's styles and gained awareness about the importance of working as a team. They also created a great action plan for what they were going to do to follow through on their team-building experience. The most common feedback I received was, "The team-building effort not only moved us forward as a team but also gave me skills I can use with my family." It felt great to get such fantastic results.

Three months later, I had an appointment with the CEO of the leadership team I had worked with. On my way to their office, I ran into one team member after another, since they were all residing in the Executive Suite. Each person greeted me with open arms and an acknowledgment of the positive team-building experience I delivered. I was on cloud nine of ego gratification. This is exactly what I loved about being a Team-Building Facilitator!

Gina, the last person to see me before I got to the CEO's office, greeted me with the warmest hug and shared, "The Team-Building experience you led was life-changing! I am so grateful for what I became aware of, what I learned, and how I have been able to improve my relationship with my husband and teenage son!"

While my ego was given a great boost and I was feeling very successful, I was surprised that Gina didn't mention the leadership team, so I asked, "I'm glad you're finding relationship success with your family, but how is your team doing since we last met?"

Gina quickly responded, "Oh, we all loved your program, but within a few weeks we went back to our old habits, and now we're just as dysfunctional as ever."

I was in shock as self-judgment kicked in, and I concluded that I was a complete failure at building teams that produced sustainable results. While I loved receiving praise and great evaluations, I measured my success by the degree to which the teams I worked with were able to achieve lasting results ... and on this front, I had failed!

INFORMAL EDUCATION—WHAT BUSINESS TEAMS CAN LEARN FROM SPORTS TEAMS

From the age of nine to twenty, I played on eight different baseball teams, four of which came in first place within our league. From the age of thirteen to the age of twenty-four, I played in nine different musical groups, including two honor bands for all of Southern California, two bands that won first place in competitions against other schools, and a rock band that won first place at the Hollywood Bowl Battle of the Bands.

Not once did I think about my vast experience participating on winning teams while getting my Master's Degree, and not once did I think of my experience on teams during the five years I spent building business teams professionally. It wasn't until 1983, when my failure to get sustainable results for my clients caused an existential crisis within me, that I began to reflect on my own personal experience on teams. Now I was forced to dig deep and study all of the ways the teams I had facilitated struggled afterward. After two years of researching all the teams I had worked with, I was able to identify one common breakdown within every team, regardless of industry, level of leadership, or size of the team. None of the teams failed to sustain results because of relationship breakdowns, lack of clear direction, or lack of trust. The single cause of breakdown common to every single team was an inability to keep commitments and follow through on agreements—in other words, a lack of accountability.

Suddenly, I had a major aha moment! Accountability only breaks down during team execution. It doesn't break down during planning, or during relationship building, and not even when resolving conflict. All team breakdowns, whether they're relationship based, trust based, task based, or results based, begin with an accountability breakdown during execution. This was a huge revelation. Accountability during execution was the domino! When accountability breaks down, so does trust. When accountability breaks down, so does performance. When accountability breaks down, so do Team Relationships. Ultimately, when there is a lack of accountability, everyone ends up working harder, struggling more, and blaming each other until burnout sets in and relationships are damaged.

But how was I supposed to get my clients to be accountable for their commitments? How was I supposed to make sure they followed through after our team-building session was over? This question led to my biggest aha moment of the time.

In all of the top-performing baseball teams, symphonies, or bands that I was fortunate to be a part of growing up, we never became a winning team by focusing on relationships. There were NO styles inventories to help us understand each other's differences. There were NO communication skill building or development of conflict-management skills. We NEVER spent time building trust, solving team puzzles, or having fun on a ropes course.

At the same time, we never focused on desired outcomes, individual metrics, or hero accomplishments either. Not once!

Instead, we always started with a clear understanding of the purpose of our team. In baseball, the coach began by sharing his vision for the team and the kind of team we were going to focus on becoming ... a hitting team or a pitching team or a team that revolved around a few key players. In each music group it was the same. We were given a clear purpose for our group—to play a certain style of music or to prepare for a particular performance or recording.

Based on our purpose, our focus and time were spent solely on team execution. No matter how effective we became, no matter how many wins or losses we received, no matter how many times we performed in front of a live audience as a music group, we continued to practice our execution as a team.

We studied, practiced, rehearsed, and reviewed our team execution over and over and over again. Whether turning a double play, running bases, or fielding a fly with people on base, we practiced team execution until we developed the highest-performing Team Habits that we could consistently execute regardless of pressure, stress, or a response to an unplanned event.

It was our team execution, our Team Habits, and our accountability to one another (not to the coach or musical director) that built our trust, shaped our communication, and led our decision-making. Team members' preferred style and opinions never shaped our execution, even though the coach or musical director was open to feedback.

While we practiced being the best we could be, we never had to be perfect because we always planned and prepared for breakdowns. We practiced "proactive recovery" as much as we planned to perform perfectly. We were prepared for anything!

It wasn't good enough to have great skills or know the baseball play or piece of music. For each baseball team, we focused on timing, sensing skills, and speed to become the best. For each music group, we focused on timing, sensing skills, and listening to each other for optimal performance.

When an individual made a mistake or caused a breakdown, we didn't blame the person. We all practiced together in support of building that team member's individual skill and team execution. We all worked hard individually to improve our skills, but we always came back to our team, orchestra, or band to ensure the highest level of team execution and performance. Team Habits, not individual stars, won games.

In *The Last Dance*, an HBO documentary about the Chicago Bulls and Michael Jordan, we learn that when Michael Jordan first became a member of the Bulls, they centered all the plays around him. And they won more games. In fact, they won their division several times in a row. But they never won the NBA Championship. When Phil Jackson was hired as the coach, he transformed the Bulls from centering around Michael Jordan to operating more as a unified team that used the various talents of several players, including Michael Jordan. The next year, they won the NBA Championship and continued winning for three years in a row.

Now, you might be saying, "But Mark, business teams are different from sports teams and music groups," and you're right. Business teams are more complex, involve more people, and never have an off-season in which they can rehearse or practice. And while that sounds like a good rationale for excusing business teams from acting more like sports teams or music groups, I'm not ready to let them off the hook just yet. Take meetings, for example. Meetings should be the vehicle for practicing team execution, but currently, they're used for unnecessary information sharing and are often perceived as overscheduled and a waste of time. In fact, 30% of the information shared in any given meeting is a repeat of information shared in another meeting!

Answer this for yourself: How many meetings are spent listening to presentations, sharing information, and tracking metrics until people's eyes glaze over or they pull out their phones to handle more pressing emails or texts? How often do you leave team meetings without ever talking about improving team execution, coordination, problem solving, or making decisions? Can you imagine how much teams would improve if they spent as much time in meetings solving problems and removing breakdowns as they do sharing information, debating different opinions, or listening to presentations? My perspective is that, yes, businesses are more complex than sports teams or music groups, and that is exactly the reason that they should spend more time optimizing team execution rather than hoping it will magically come together. Greater complexity means a greater number of potential breakdowns, so it's only logical that greater emphasis on team execution should be made to address those complexities. The more linkages that exist, the greater the chance of weakness and failure.

THE TEST TRIAL

In 1985, I revamped my team-building process to start with purpose, just like every sports team and music group I'd been a part of. Then, our time was spent sorting out effective execution, including Team Habits, role clarification, and how the team could hold themselves and each other accountable. Once the team agreed upon, developed, and measured optimal Team Habits to achieve their desired outcomes, only *then* did we focus on relationships. Why? Because relationships are already being built and changed in real time as the team members turn their focus to their desired business outcomes and the Team Habits necessary for optimal performance and communication. When business outcomes take precedence, there's no need to focus up front on making people comfortable or happy.

By the time we focus solely on Team Relationships based on the original assessment, they have already transformed. In fact, the trust, support, and effective communication that is at the heart of effective relationships was already developed while the team developed their purpose, Team Habits, and priorities for tracking outcomes and improvement.

The first team to go through this new team process was a Critical Care Nursing Unit of a medical center in Southern California. The head nurse of that unit was on a Performance Plan (in those days called corrective action) because she was not performing well and had several complaints from her nursing unit. Because she was a long-term employee of the medical center, they had to give her six months to turn her performance around. She asked for my assistance, since I also delivered management training for the organization. The organization had a top-down approach to leadership and were not proponents of team-building efforts, but they agreed to the head nurse's request, to demonstrate that they did everything to support her before they let her go.

The head nurse was a poor communicator and didn't have the trust of her four charge nurses, and the nurses in the Critical Care area complained about her poor leadership. Instead of focusing on building trust, improving relationships, and solving the conflicts that existed, we started with getting an aligned purpose for their leadership team and for the reputation that they wanted the Critical Care Nursing Unit to have with patients, other departments, and executives.

Then, we developed a set of Team Habits for how they would collectively lead the nursing unit, which included agreed-upon behaviors for scheduling nurses, improving quality, responding to problems, making decisions, and communicating those decisions to others. At the end of the session, we created a couple of agreements to support their relationships with one another and established a team plan for communicating with the rest of the nursing unit. Finally, the management team developed a clear process for follow-up in their team meetings with continual assessment of how well they performed based on commitments made. By the end of the team session, the charge nurses expressed full support for the head nurse—for the first time in months!

Within three months, the performance and morale of the Critical Care Nursing Unit improved so much that the executives had to remove the head nurse from her Performance Plan. Other nursing units noticed the difference in the Critical Care Team, and three other nursing units requested of executives that they receive the same Team-Building Process. The head nurse went from being on a Performance Plan to being one of the top head nurses in the organization within six months. Even though senior management approved other nursing departments going through my Team-Building Process, they would never admit the value of teamwork for the entire organization. However, each nursing unit improved in a similar way and cross-functional nursing unit support also improved.

Three years later, the head nurse of the Critical Care Nursing Unit left the medical center for a higher-level leadership role in a different industry, and the management team made sure to hire the next head nurse who would continue the Team-Building Process that I had originally set up for them three years earlier.

The focus on team execution and supportive accountability rather than a culture of blame demonstrated the success I had envisioned back in 1983 when I wasn't able to get the long-lasting results I wanted from the teams I was working with.

In Chapter 2, you will learn the myths that I had to overcome in order to discover and optimize the missing piece to building teams that traditional Organizational Development has neglected for over fifty years.

2

BREAKING THE RULES
FOR BUILDING TEAMS

"The secret of change is to focus all of your energy, not on
fighting the old, but on building the new."
— Dan Millman

THE IMPOSSIBLE GOAL

Tom was the CIO of a 2,000-person Information Systems department of
a global manufacturing company based in France. He was given three and
a half years by the CEO to centralize his department—a department that
consisted of over sixty plants in seventeen countries across four continents.
This was not going to be an easy task, so Tom brought us in on recommendation from one of his advisors to determine if our unique approach
to rapid team building and business transformation could work to resolve
their time-sensitive transformation.

Tom led our first meeting.

"We've been trying to transition our department from being decentralized to centralized, and after two years, we haven't made any progress,"
he told me. "Now I only have one and a half years to complete the transition, or our CEO will outsource our entire IS department, like one of our
competitors did a few years ago." He was distraught.

"What have you done so far to make the change?" I asked.

Deflated and exasperated, he shared that a top consulting organization had created a road map for the change, starting with team building for senior leadership to ensure they were aligned. They then implemented a series of leadership and project management training programs to provide the skills necessary to make the change.

"That all sounds really good," I said. "You provided the clarity, the alignment, and the support to make it happen. So, what went wrong?"

"My leadership team members all have different functions and even different locations," he shared. "They all claim to be aligned on the purpose and the plan, but when it comes to implementation, none of them want to give up their autonomy to integrate our department. They are afraid of not satisfying their internal manufacturing plant customer." He looked defeated. "I am completely frustrated by my leadership team and don't have a solution." With skepticism in his voice, he continued, "I was told you use a different approach to creating a significant change that doesn't depend on my Senior Leadership Team needing to take charge."

"That's correct," I told him. Ultimately, it's middle management who leads the execution of change, not senior management. However, it *only* works when they lead as a unified and aligned middle management team, not as fragmented leaders in functional silos.

Tom interrupted, "Wait a minute. We have around sixty-five people in middle management and key project leadership roles. How do you plan to build a team with that many people? That goes against everything I have ever read about effective team building!"

Tom wasn't wrong. Conventional wisdom says you can't do team building with more than twenty-five people, and building a team out of middle management leaders and relying on them to lead a massive organizational change *does* go against the common paradigm of effective team building. And that's exactly why it works.

SIX TEAM-BUILDING RULES THAT NEED BREAKING

Our beliefs shape our reality. But where do we learn the thoughts that form our beliefs? Most of them are taught to us as rules by parents, friends, teachers, and perceived "experts," while other beliefs are developed from our experience. The problem is, most of us go through life looking for evidence that the beliefs we already hold are true! This means that the beliefs we develop from our experience often mirror the beliefs we're taught, even if they're totally false. This can leave us stuck in limiting beliefs that hold us back or cause us to make the same mistakes over and over again, all the while expecting new and different results each time. Frustrating, isn't it?

There were several rules that I was taught about building effective teams that I didn't challenge until my shocking failure in 1983. Some of these included the following:

- The ideal size of a team is between eight and twelve people. Today, it's more common to think that the ideal size of a team is between fifteen and twenty-five people at the most. (Spoiler: still false!)
- People have to trust one another before they can bond as a team.
- Team members have to buy into being part of a team in order to support other team members.
- All teams experience four common stages of team development: Forming, Storming, Norming, and Performing. This is based on the work of Bruce Tuckman.

Over time, I've had to question and let go of many strongly held beliefs and rules about effective team building in favor of *actually* building effective teams. This was not easy; some of these rules I was very attached to! But ultimately, if we want results, we have to be willing to trade out what we believe reality to be for what reality actually is.

Old Rule #1: You can build a team "off the field."
New Rule: You can only build the team "on the field."

Remember Gina from Chapter 1? When I went back to her team and asked them what had happened, she explained it quite clearly.

"When we were at the hotel on retreat, all of our defenses were down. It was great to let our hair down and get personal with each other. The activities you had us do enhanced our empathy for each other, improved our communication, and taught us the value of teamwork. But when we got back to the workplace, our competing functional priorities took over, along with our fight for limited resources. The breakdowns that occurred between departments resulted in the same old blame and defensive posturing. Some of us are individually getting along with each other better, but we aren't working better as a team."

This is one of the biggest problems I see with conventional team building. It's done off site, away from the workplace, and has nothing to do with the kind of teamwork needed to actually perform the job!

Professional athletes build their teams "on the field," playing their real positions and executing their plays. They don't just talk about it, align on values, play games, or solve case studies to simulate playing together. They learn to communicate, coordinate, solve problems, and make decisions by doing the work of practicing their actual plays. This forces team members to face real challenges, obstacles, and personal differences that will show up in the live game.

If professional sports teams learn on the field, why shouldn't other professions as well? Ultimately, the team-building experience from start to finish must reflect real obstacles, real challenges, real communication, and real problem solving in order to stick well enough to be replicated "in the game," or, as business would call it—in the workplace.

Old Rule #2: All teams must follow the same stages of development.

New Rule: All teams are developed differently based on their purpose, desired outcomes, and constraints.

A medical center had challenges in two different departments—the Emergency Department and the Rehabilitation Department. Whenever I work with a team, the session I create for them depends on their desired outcomes and constraints. I quickly learned that the two departments not only had different desired outcomes and constraints, they were literally opposite to each other! While traditional team building would tell you that the two departments should have these things in common as part of the same medical center, an approach based on that assumption would be doomed to fail. Their differences meant that they needed to communicate differently, coordinate differently, plan differently, make decisions differently, and track results differently.

The purpose of the Emergency Department was mostly to save patients. Urgent and decisive decision-making was critical and led by physicians and registered nurses. There was no time for inclusive feedback, discussion and debate, or getting consensus for the next actions taken.

The Rehabilitation Department's purpose was recovery, which they accomplished in a very deliberate manner over multiple weeks. This required input, discussion, and consensual decision-making from the physician, physical therapist, occupational therapist, and sometimes other involved healthcare providers as needed.

Every team has a unique purpose, desired outcomes, and conditions for operating. Because of this, building teams is an individualized endeavor; there is no one-size-fits-all approach. Developing executive, middle management, department, project, and self-managed teams all must be treated differently to ensure successful results. And this even goes further for teams that operate within one building, those that are spread across a huge campus of buildings, those in different cities within the same country, and those spread across multiple time zones in different countries, cultures, and business norms.

Old Rule #3: The ideal size of a team is under twenty-five people.

New Rule: The ideal size of a team is determined by the number of people who need to coordinate, solve problems, and make decisions together to optimize performance.

You'd be hard-pressed to find a study that didn't agree that the ideal size of a team is between twelve and twenty-five people. Experts believe that this number of people best optimizes diversity, participation, and solving problems. But what if it's the common team-building approach, not team building itself, that limits the number of people who can be effective on a team? What if there was a team-building approach that could optimize how thirty-five, fifty, or even sixty-five people came together to achieve their particular purpose and desired outcomes? While most facilitators believe this to be impossible, my team of consultants and I have consistently witnessed teams of this size improving execution by 60% to 80%, improving Team Relationships by 15% to 35% based on fifteen attributes of team effectiveness, and accomplishing their business outcomes on time or ahead of schedule.

The manager of a department in a municipality wanted to develop her team, which operated in a very siloed way. When we met, Ruth shared with me that all of her five functional areas were siloed, but getting all of the directors and managers together to create more of a unified team would mean getting forty-five to fifty people in the room together.

I responded, "Ruth, I can easily work with forty-five people in the same team-building effort, especially if the departments impact each other."

"They do, but there are really three of the five departments that are critical for working together, and that would drop the number to about twenty-five people, which is closer to the ideal size of a team," she insisted.

At the afternoon break of the first day of our team session with her twenty-five, Ruth took me aside.

"I made a big mistake!" she lamented. "You said your process was different, but I didn't understand it until I experienced it. Now, I can see why you wanted to have everyone in the same room at the same time. I really wished I had gone with your idea of getting all forty-five leaders together. Please think about what we can do to integrate them into the team afterward, because your process is creating the transformation, in only one day, that I thought would have taken the complete two days to achieve."

While it's easier to build a team of twenty-five people than a team of fifty people, it's impossible to build a team of fifty people by only including twenty-five of them.

Old Rule #4: Teams are developed during a team-building event that resolves breakdowns and improves performance.

New Rule: Teams evolve over time as team members change, as they function at higher levels, and as the business environment changes.

Jim was the new president of a Senior Leadership Team for a business unit in a large corporation. He was challenged by poor quality, safety, and customer satisfaction scores.

Jim shared, "We have great talent and great working conditions, but everyone takes it for granted. Employees are dissatisfied, and our key metrics are lower than other business units. They hired me to turn around this situation, but I need the alignment of every executive if we are going to be successful. Unfortunately, each executive is more interested in protecting their own area than making changes to support the organization as a whole."

Because the business unit had about 1,800 employees and needed a culture change to shift people's mindsets and behaviors, it was expected to take three to five years to turn the situation around.

After one and a half years, the business unit had increased all of their metrics except for customer satisfaction. Employee engagement went from an average of 25% to an average of 70%, according to their engagement survey, and involvement in employee activities reached as much as 80% participation.

The Senior Leadership Team improved their execution as a team by 73% and Team Relationships improved by an average of 30%, according to fifteen areas that measure Team Relationships. They were functioning super well, but in October of that second year, the President contacted me and shared the news.

With a worried look, Jim said, "Corporate has decided to centralize all of the business units, so we are losing our autonomy. This changes everything because they are very autocratic and Counter-Culture to how we have improved our business unit. I'm not sure how we will make the shift."

"No worries," I smiled. "All we need to do is create a new Picture of Success and develop new Team Habits for Collective Execution based on these new conditions. I trust that your team will be able to figure this out and establish a new way to operate with the new corporate direction."

"But what about all of the habits we developed that turned around the culture and performance of the organization?" he continued. "I don't want to lose what we created."

"Don't worry!" I confidently responded. "We will build on those habits, and they'll actually help you make the shift even faster."

We brought the Senior Leadership Team together and assessed all of their current Team Habits for Collective Execution. Not only had they ingrained those habits, but they also had determined that they had to create seven new Team Habits that would assist them in the transformation. They also created a habit around improving employee engagement to find solutions for improving customer satisfaction.

Both sports teams and music groups evolve over time as their customers and fans evolve, as the industry gets more competitive, as technology improves, and as markets change.

Therefore, effective and sustainable team building is less about creating an event and more about setting teams up with a system for evolution that can be tracked, measured, and modified as conditions continually change.

Old Rule #5: Team accountability means no one is really accountable.

New Rule: Team accountability and Shared Ownership increase individual accountability and accelerate informed decision-making.

When I played baseball, I was afraid of dropping the ball or making an error, but not because I might be yelled at by the coach (which he did in front of everyone). I was afraid of letting my teammates down. I didn't want to be the cause of us losing a game or putting us at risk for losing a game.

I learned very early in life that I felt more pressured by and accountable to my teammates and peers than I did to the coach.

I also felt supported by my teammates. As a high school pitcher, when my rhythm was off and I couldn't throw a strike to save my life, five different team members offered to play "catcher" for me over the weekend to help me get my rhythm back. These weren't just my closest friends on the team. Some I didn't know very well at all, and one was another pitcher who would have seen more action if my performance stayed poor.

That experience demonstrated team accountability—the practice of not allowing any team member to play at less than their capability. It also demonstrated Shared Ownership, where team members support one another in solving problems or removing obstacles that could prevent the success of the team. My teammates could have let me struggle, blamed me for doing a poor job, or expected me to improve my performance on my own, since pitching was my role and responsibility. But instead they came together to support me for the good of the team as a whole and our desire to win games.

Team accountability means that you are not only accountable for your individual role on the team, but you are also accountable for contributing to the success of the team. This means that you not only need to achieve excellence in your role to support top performance of your team, but you also must do whatever is takes to support other team members or solve challenges and ensure team success. Supporting the team is *never* an excuse for not performing your role, unless the team and team leader agree with that shift.

Shared Ownership for achieving the team's top priorities and outcomes doesn't mean that every team member is involved with every decision or needs to approve every change made by the team to achieve its outcomes. Shared Ownership means that you contribute to solving any problem on the team or removing any obstacle that prevents team success whether it involves your particular role or not.

A large medical corporation was planning to open up a new facility about twenty miles away from the current one. To open, they needed to fill 2,000 positions. Unfortunately, about four months prior to opening, the department that was in charge of filling those 2,000 positions was behind on meeting their goal. Instead of being blamed by anyone on the eighteen-person extended leadership team, they all got involved in creating innovative solutions.

They could have just pushed back the opening date, but instead each member of the team decided to add recruitment to their role and accelerate the hiring process.

Four months later, the 2,000-person facility opened on time with only two positions open—a huge success for the entire leadership team.

Old Rule #6: You can only build a team with an in-person session.
New Rule: You can effectively build a team in a virtual session.

When leadership training programs were becoming popular in online formats, I was asked by an instructional designer, "Do you think it's possible to conduct your team-building program in an online virtual environment?"

I was absolutely clear and emphatic in my response: "Absolutely NOT!"

Annoyed at the suggestion, I continued with my explanation. "It's impossible to build a team without being in person due to the dynamics on the team, the lack of connection between team members, and the stale environment of the virtual world. How could you possibly have meaningful discussion, debate, and effective resolution when each team member is in a different location? It's just not practical, so it's never going to happen!"

Then, the pandemic came upon us, and all of my team-building engagements immediately disappeared as my clients canceled, one after the other. Sometimes, when our beliefs are entrenched, life deals us an unsuspecting blow to challenge our paradigm.

It took three months and about ten people on my team to figure out how to transform our highly effective and results-producing team sessions into a virtual format. We tested the program several times to make sure that we could run the program smoothly, provide the same level of team interaction that we currently provided, address virtual fatigue, and ensure the kind of transformation that we were used to accomplishing with our clients.

Within one year, we conducted almost ten different team-building sessions with executive teams, middle management teams, department teams, and project teams. As expected, some clients were extremely reluctant to try a virtual format, but they too had no choice if they wanted to progress.

Not only did virtual team building work well with our clients, but there also were many advantages that we discovered, including the following:

- Teams had a much easier time transitioning from the team-building workshop to their workplace setting because now most of their interaction and meetings were conducted virtually.
- Documentation to track commitments, agreements, and project plans were much faster and easier in a virtual environment because we didn't have to translate from flip charts to electronic forms.
- The team's dynamics were much less dominated by the few who like to speak up, since the virtual tools of chat, the use of calling on people to open their mics, and everyone being on screen in an equal way, without the normal dominating presence of some team members, allowed for more participation from those usually less talkative in team meetings.
- Finally, it allowed everyone to participate from all over the country, and in one case from around the world, without having the resource cost and travel time for the organization.

Many people think that I came up with this different approach to building teams by studying different team-building methodologies. The reality is that I am a practitioner at heart, and I am very dedicated to getting results for my clients. If my beliefs are in the way of getting results, then I question and challenge my way of doing things, regardless of how many experts say it is the "correct" way. And many times, my learning comes from mistakes and being challenged by my own misunderstandings, as in the case of needing to go virtual or go out of business.

ACHIEVING THE IMPOSSIBLE

Tom, the CIO of the multinational manufacturing organization from earlier in the chapter, was extremely nervous about having only eighteen months to centralize his department of sixty-plus manufacturing plants in seventeen countries.

He was now face to face with sixty members of the senior and middle management extended leadership team who showed up from all over the world. It was definitely overwhelming, and he wasn't sure it was going to work.

Utilizing small group processes, the middle management team developed and agreed to a clear Picture of Success for leading the change to centralization. They also created twenty Team Habits that described how they would plan various projects in the supply chain, inclusively solve problems in a practical way across multiple time zones and entities, make decisions without going to senior management, and effectively share information and communicate across multiple time zones and various functions.

In addition, we identified and planned the major projects necessary to make the change as well as the biggest concerns and challenges to completing those projects with recovery plans in place.

What we didn't do was have them play games, do a ropes course, or discuss their Team Relationships outside of what was needed for developing new Team Habits.

By the end of the three days, they were not only clear on next steps but also developed a meeting structure to ensure follow-up accountability, problem solving, and decision-making.

On the last day, Tom shared with me that this was the first time he'd experienced a team-building program that focused solely on team execution for his real business challenges during every stage of the process. Instead of focusing on relationships, the team used their desired outcomes as a team to define their Team Relationships. "It was so seamless," Tom told me. "I finally get how your process works and why it's so unique."

The group of senior and middle managers were brought back after six months to measure results. While all of their measures improved and their project outcomes were on schedule, it was felt by the team that they needed to move to a higher level of team performance. So, we used our time together to have them identify what changes they would make in their Team Habits, their project processes, and their ways of holding each other accountable to raise their standards of leadership.

Three months later, we met again, but this was more of a celebration. In just nine months, they had achieved centralization—a feat that was expected to take eighteen months. They also improved their KPIs by 50% and saved the organization tens of millions of dollars. Finally, all six of their prioritized IS projects were on schedule and met their internal customer's quality expectations—an outcome they had never previously achieved. And they did this on their own without spending $200,000 per project getting support from another external consultant they used regularly.

We broke all the rules and achieved the impossible!

In the next chapter, you will learn exactly why team building that focuses on interpersonal relationships and styles is a waste of time and the root cause of why Team Relationships break down. It's so compelling, you'll wonder why we've spent decades wasting time and money trying to build teams the old way.

3

A CONTRARIAN APPROACH TO BUILDING EFFECTIVE TEAMS

"It doesn't matter where you are coming from. All that matters
is where you are going."

—Brian Tracy

BROKEN TRUST, BAD RELATIONSHIPS, BUSINESS FAILURE

Judy was the division manager for a multi-plant, German-based manufacturing organization operating in the United States. She called me in for a consult because she had the lowest-performing plant with the lowest morale in the United States. It was an embarrassment to her and to Corporate, which had given her and the other leaders until the end of the year to get their act together. Otherwise, they'd be replaced.

She attributed the low performance and morale to the lack of trust and collaboration between their three primary departments—Operations, Quality, and Maintenance. "Their relationships are completely broken," she said. The leaders of each department blamed each other for breakdowns, failed to include each other when they planned new projects, were constantly in conflict, and demonstrated a lack of respect when they were in the same meetings. It sounded bad.

In an attempt to address these issues, she'd already provided training programs for all three directors, including conducting difficult conversations and managing conflict. They even had each manager complete a communications-style assessment with coaching to better understand each one's style of communication.

"There was improvement for only a short time," she admitted, sounding defeated. The three directors had agreed that it would be good for building their relationships to cook and eat dinner together. This solution matched their organizational core value of engaging employees in problem solving, and this would give them the opportunity to depend on each other, support each other, and socialize together in order to let down their antagonism and build trust between them. While it sounded like a good idea and seemed like a great success at first, soon they were back to their old conflicts, blame-game antics, and lack of trust.

"It's impressive how much effort you have put into solving this breakdown," I told her. "But I'm not surprised it didn't work."

Leaders often try to solve problems within their teams by focusing on the *symptom*, rather than the *source* of the breakdown. It's the most common misunderstanding known to building teams!

COMMON-SENSE TEAM BUILDING

Think about every college or professional sports team, music group, or dance company you may have participated in. How many of them built their teams by socializing, making meals together, or doing any other form of team-building activities to solidify their teamwork and relationships?

That's right. None of them.

Music groups, sports teams, and dance companies are under intense pressure and take a huge risk when they perform in front of thousands of people. If they don't gel as a team, they simply won't make it professionally. And yet, they never do team-building activities like cooking dinner together with the expectation that it will improve their performance and execution on stage or on the field. If these professional teams, whose job depends almost entirely on teamwork, don't do team building this way, why do business teams?

The truth is that business teams and organizations, just like sports teams and music groups, don't align and execute on business goals by developing or teaching values and principles, nor do they achieve business goals by building trusting relationships. They build alignment and achieve their outcomes by agreeing on four Success Factors, in the following order.

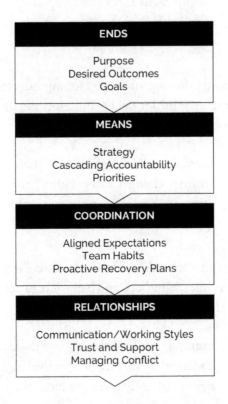

Figure 1 Clarifying ENDS, MEANS, COORDINATION, and RELATIONSHIPS

THE ENDS IS THE BEGINNING

In *The Seven Habits of Highly Effective People*, Dr. Stephen Covey's second habit is this: Begin with the end in mind. For business teams and organizations, the ENDS refers to Purpose, Desired Results, and Ideal Transformation of both the business and the culture.

The ENDS represents *what* we are going to accomplish and is answered by asking the following three questions to clarify the team's direction:

- What is our purpose as a team in supporting our internal or external customers and the goals of our organization during the next year?

    o Example: An HR Leadership Team wanted to be seen as valuable business partners with the business leaders they were supporting.

- What results do we need to accomplish that will provide game-changing value for the organization and for our team's effectiveness and efficiency?

    o Example: More effectively strategize and execute business changes to optimize fast results and culture shifts, rather than only raise objections based on "protecting the organization."

- What transformation do we need to make collectively and individually in our roles, mindsets, and behaviors to achieve our purpose and breakthrough (B STATE) results?

    o Example: Shift from being HR leaders to business leaders with an HR perspective, and become change agents rather than change blockers.

THE MEANS MAKES YOUR ENDS REAL

Based on your ENDS, the next step is clarifying the MEANS.

The MEANS represents the strategy, priorities, and specific goals for accomplishing the ENDS. The MEANS is usually taken care of by the organization's Strategic Plan and includes their process of setting priorities that cascade down the organization. The MEANS includes the strategy for growing revenue, increasing profitability, investing in capital expenditures to improve equipment, and developing human capability for improving organizational performance. The MEANS clarifies the approach for accomplishing the purpose, desired results, and transformation.

COORDINATION IS THE HEART OF MANIFESTATION

The next word in this model is COORDINATION. While ENDS and MEANS represent *what* the team intends to accomplish, COORDINATION represents *how* the team will achieve their accomplishment in the optimal manner. One of the most common ways organizations improve coordination is by implementing RASCI processes that clarify Responsibility, Accountability, Support, Consultation, and Information between multiple functions involved in a particular process to deliver business results. This supports more effective decision-making and communication among different team members. While RASCI is a good start for clarifying *what* people's roles are on a team, it doesn't describe *how* individuals will *collectively execute* with each other to optimize business results.

COORDINATION represents the optimal *Collective Execution* necessary to effectively and efficiently take action for achieving the MEANS. It not only represents roles, responsibilities, and expectations for various team members but also their Team Habits (not individual habits) to optimize planning, coordination, information sharing, decision-making, problem solving, and messaging to others.

It's this stage of the process that sports teams and music groups spend 90% of their time in. It's their practice or rehearsal. There is a strong correlation between practice effectiveness and game-time performance. Team Habits in a business setting represent how the team will optimize their execution of processes, procedures, and skills in an aligned way to boost their speed, quality, adaptability, and responsiveness, as well as their recovery when things don't go as planned.

RELATIONSHIPS GET BACK TO EACH INDIVIDUAL

The final stage in this process is RELATIONSHIPS.

RELATIONSHIPS refer to trust, support, styles, communication, managing conflict between team members, and individual accountability. It depicts how team members get along with each other, relate to each other, and respect each other during their interactions.

The process begins at the top and works its way down.

As I explained this model to Judy, she piped in here with a little impatience, "This all makes sense, but I am not sure what this model has to do with my troubled plant that is clearly broken at the relationship level of trust, support, communication, and managing conflict."

THE BIG REVEAL

"Glad you asked, Judy!" This was my favorite part of the model—the big reveal.

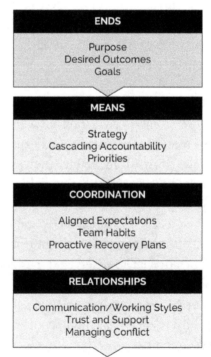

Figure 2   Breakdown at the ENDS causing MEANS, COORDINATION, and RELATIONSHIP breakdowns

The magical thing about this model is, if a team isn't aligned on the ENDS, by definition they will be in conflict about the MEANS for achieving the ENDS, the COORDINATION to accomplish their MEANS, and their RELATIONSHIPS that will result in mistrust and conflicts. However, if the team is aligned on their ENDS but isn't aligned on their MEANS, then everything below the MEANS will also be in conflict.

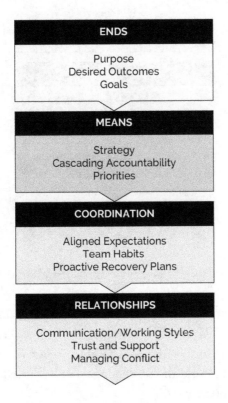

Figure 3 Breakdown at the MEANS causing COORDINATION and RELATIONSHIP breakdowns

In other words, if the team agrees on their purpose but doesn't agree on the priorities for achieving their purpose, then their COORDINATION will be in conflict, and that will result in trust issues in the RELATIONSHIPS phase of the model.

If the ENDS and MEANS are both in alignment, that is even better.

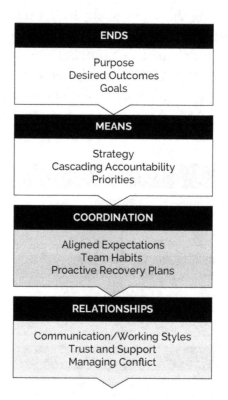

Figure 4 Breakdown at COORDINATION causing RELATIONSHIP breakdowns

But if they aren't aligned and clear on how they will collectively execute as part of the COORDINATION phase, they will also end up with trust issues and conflicts in the RELATIONSHIP phase of the model. It's all very logical as you look at the consequences of having a lack of alignment anywhere in the four phases.

I turned to Judy. "I have a question for you," I said in a devious tone. "Given all of the different scenarios I just described where breakdowns

CAN take place, where is the one phase in which a breakdown always shows itself?"

Judy responded without hesitation, "RELATIONSHIPS!"

No matter where there is a breakdown, it will always show up as a RELATIONSHIP issue, when in fact, most often the root cause is somewhere in the ENDS, MEANS, or COORDINATION. Thus, we end up solving for the symptom of the problem, not the root cause. Even if some relationship issues resolve through team building, it will be temporary if you don't address the lack of alignment at the higher phases in the model.

"Wow," Judy responded, stunned. "So all of this time, we were addressing the shiny object of RELATIONSHIPS when the real issue is a lack of understanding or alignment at the ENDS, MEANS, or COORDINATION levels."

"Yes," I confirmed. "But there is one more interesting trap that most organizations and teams fall into that gives us even more insight into this process."

Now, Judy couldn't wait for me to share the next part of the reveal.

"Generally speaking," I said, "most organizations are really good at describing the ENDS—their purpose, desired outcomes and sometimes even the transformation needed." I circled the ENDS on the whiteboard and continued. "But when it comes to MEANS, organizations start to have difficulty." Typically, organizations are good at creating their Strategic Plan, but they tend to be ineffective at clarifying priorities. Either they make everything a priority, put a multitude of priorities in "pillars," or constantly change priorities throughout the year. This leads to a constant state of confusion, overwhelm, and crisis.

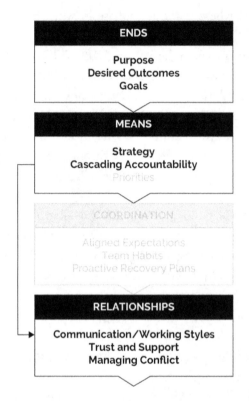

Figure 5 Moving from Means to Relationships and Missing Priority Clarification and COORDINATION

Organizations rarely address the COORDINATION phase except to develop processes, but with no agreement on how they will collectively execute to optimize results. Once they have their Strategic Plan, they go directly to RELATIONSHIPS to solve conflicts and hold individuals accountable.

As a consultant, it's easy for me to diagnose any organizational breakdown by starting at the ENDS and working my way down the four phases to find out where the highest point in the model is where there is a lack of clarity or alignment. That tells me exactly where to start with the team or organizational change effort.

People think I am so fast at diagnosing the root cause of organizational breakdowns like it's a magic trick. Truthfully, it's just a common-sense logical progression. Most leaders and consultants just miss it because they are so focused on trying to fix relationships!

FIXING BROKEN RELATIONSHIPS WITHOUT DISCUSSING RELATIONSHIPS

Judy was right about her plant, except it was even worse than I was expecting. Not only did they have conflicts between the Operations, Quality, and Maintenance departments, but they also had complete polarization. Before coming to the offsite, each director and his ten leadership team members had prepared a formalized strategy to attack the other departments during the offsite.

Even though the situation was in such a dire and extreme state, Judy could only afford the time and the budget to give me one day with the thirty-person leadership team—only one day to transform a large group of people committed to blaming one another for the breakdowns the plant was facing.

Following the model I'd laid out to Judy, I started by asking the entire group about their ENDS, including what they needed to accomplish during the next year. Different people from all three teams responded without hesitation.

- Improve our quality performance as a plant, since we are the lowest performers in the U.S.
- Improve our productivity, since we are missing schedules
- Improve morale, which is also the lowest of all the plants
- Effectively plan an equipment replacement project that will cause a temporary shutdown of the plant and cost over $125M

"Of the four outcomes you need to accomplish," I asked, "which is the biggest risk for you as a leadership team?"

Two different team members agreed from different sides of the room. "The equipment replacement project is our biggest risk. It's a very difficult equipment upgrade, and if we're late, it could cost the organization millions of dollars."

"Does anyone disagree with what's been shared as your deliverables and your most at-risk project?" I asked to confirm alignment of the ENDS and even the major priority of the four projects representing the MEANS.

I heard voices from all three departments agree—maybe the first time they had agreed on anything in months!

I tracked their four projects, circling the equipment replacement project as their agreed-upon focus and priority.

"Let's now focus on translating that aligned direction into optimizing how to get it done on time and on budget," I continued. "But here is how this will work. I need you to pretend we have a clean slate ... starting over ... and imagine what will be necessary to optimize your functioning with each other to achieve this project, without thinking of any history that has derailed you in the past. My job is to ask you questions and challenge your responses to make sure it makes sense and that you are aligned.

"You will have to create a project plan for leading this project," I told them. "How will you need to do that differently than you've done it in the past so that you can optimize your results?" I asked to get us started.

Immediately someone spoke up, "We need to plan this with representatives from all three functional areas: Operations, Maintenance, and Quality."

"Why do you need to involve all three functional areas?" I challenged.

I was surprised when a team member from a different department responded. "Currently, one department creates a plan and then shares it with the next department to create their plan in a siloed manner. But for this project, we all impact each other, so we will need to have full representation from all three departments to produce an effective and efficient plan."

Several other team members from all three departments confirmed that approach.

"Okay," I said and continued my questioning. "How will you need to make decisions going forward to complete this challenging project?"

Again, another team member who hadn't spoken up yet responded, "We will have to represent all three departments whenever we make a decision on this project or even make a change to the project plan."

"Wow!" I exclaimed. "That seems like a lot of extra coordination and time to make decisions. Are you sure you need to do that?"

Now people were getting upset with my questioning. Several more team members got involved in the discussion to defend the proposed point of view.

"We have to include each other when making decisions," he said, "because any decision is going to have a ripple effect on the other departments. Even if they aren't directly part of making the decisions, they need to be included so that we can adjust as quickly as possible. Today, we leave each other out and make isolated decisions, which causes multiple breakdowns during implementation from lack of preparation." All three teams emphatically agreed with this point of view.

I was impressed with the teams' clear understanding of the importance of cross-functional teamwork. But it was obvious that even though they knew they needed to work cross-functionally, they didn't operate this way.

I posed a question, "You are going to have problems and breakdowns show up during the project. There's no way to get it completely right or anticipate all the situations that could go wrong. How will you handle that as a leadership team?"

One team member responded, "We have to surface any problem as soon as possible to all of the departments so that everyone is prepared to modify our plans accordingly."

Another team member added to that response, "No matter where the problem shows itself, we will need to reach out to the other departments to include them in solving the problem, because no matter what the solution is, it will have an impact on the other departments."

One more team member spoke up, "We have to make sure that we never blame another department for any problem that shows up. To achieve this project, we will need to keep a positive attitude, include each other with full transparency, and solve problems together."

As I was tracking each of their solutions on the flip chart, I stopped and asked a completely different question.

"You all seem so clear in your responses. How often do you currently function in the way that you are all describing as answers to my questions?"

Again, in full self-disclosure, another team member responded, "We have never worked this way."

"So, given that this is new, we need to clarify how this way of operating will actually work in your environment to set clear expectations." This is done by creating Team Habits that describe the process and behaviors for working collaboratively in the way you desire. Team Habits are the essential missing piece for effective COORDINATION.

We split the thirty leaders into small cross-functional groups to develop twenty Team Habits based on the previous brainstorm. Their habits included things like expectations around decision-making, planning, problem solving, information sharing, project planning, and speaking with a unified voice to others in the organization.

Everyone was getting along as if there were no conflicts. Relationship issues were completely resolved without focusing on them at all.

ONE-DAY TEAM RESULTS

By the end of our one day together, the leaders accomplished a lot by working as a cross-functional and effective team to create the following:

- A clear Picture of Success for how they were going to work together
- Twenty Team Habits to describe in detail what their COORDI-NATION phase would look like
- A baseline measurement for each of the Team Habits
- Aligned plans for improving the top five habits they agreed to focus on for the first three to five months
- A plan for developing the plan to manage their huge project
- A meeting structure that would be cross-functional to raise concerns, address problems together, and support the positive relationships on the team

At the end of the meeting, two different team members from different departments came up to me to ask a question and make a complaint. They showed me a list of grievances about the behavior of team members from other departments and asked, "We spent time preparing these lists of issues prior to our offsite, but you never allowed us to share them. When in your process do we get to talk about our grievances with the other departments?"

I responded, "Look at your list and then look at your Team Habits and plans for improvement," which were tracked on all four walls filled with completed flip charts of their work.

I continued, "Compare the two lists and tell me what you notice."

The two team members looked back and forth from their list to the walls and back to their lists again.

Almost at the same time, both team members said, "Given what we have created here as a team, our list of grievances simply won't exist. We didn't have to solve them. In the new environment, they all simply disappear."

"That's exactly right," I validated their response. "You never needed to solve the current problems. You just needed to create a new environment in which those issues won't exist."

FROM LAST TO FIRST

Within six months, the team's relationships improved by 25%, according to our fifteen-question Team Relationship Assessment, and their Team Habits improved by 70%, even though their focus was on 20% of the twenty Team Habits. Their effectiveness as a team had great results for their business:

- They improved quality, productivity, and morale to become one of the top-performing plants in the United States—a remarkably fast improvement for a group that started out in complete polarization.
- Their equipment project was completed on time and on budget for the first time in the history of the plant.

This is just one case study, but it represents what I see over and over again with my clients: team relationship problems rarely occur at the relationship level. Their roots almost always lie in the ENDS, MEANS, or COORDINATION level of interaction. In the next chapter, we'll take a deep dive into why fixing relationships won't fix your team, and you'll learn how the missing piece of developing Team Habits is critical for improving business results and Team Relationships at the same time!

4

THE MISSING PIECE

"If you are going to achieve excellence in big things, you develop the habit in the little matters. Excellence is not an exception, it is a prevailing attitude."

—Colin Powell

As we saw in the last chapter with Judy's manufacturing organization, focusing on relationships and interpersonal trust is not the key to building high-performance teams. Breakdowns will always show up in relationships even if the source of the breakdown is in misalignment of the ENDS, MEANS, or COORDINATION of a team or project. So, if it's not relationships that dictate whether or not a team will be successful, what is it?

THE TRUST FALL

Organizational leaders love to take their teams to ropes courses and escape rooms. They do trust falls, climb thirty feet out of their comfort zones, and experience teamwork that can only come from a heightened sense of danger and increased adrenaline. So, why don't these trust falls translate to better relationships and execution in the workplace?

Well, it's an easy answer, really. We're chasing the wrong kind of trust. There is a difference between *relationship trust* and *execution trust*. In fact, they're almost completely unrelated.

Relationship trust is the kind of trust we're all familiar with—it's the trust that two people build on a personal level. It's the trust you have with your work bestie and your parents and your friends that develops through shared stories, easy communication, being with each other through hard times, and fun gossip and banter. While relationship trust is nice to have with coworkers, it's not going to make the machine run. In fact, unless an organization is highly dysfunctional, there is no correlation between good Team Relationships and achieving Team Outcomes at all!

Execution trust, on the other hand, is based on setting clear expectations, meeting those expectations, and being transparent about making changes if necessary. However, when expectations aren't clear, or not kept, or changed without warning or consideration of any domino effects, then trust breaks down—along with support, communication, and the ability to resolve conflicts. This means that most relationship breakdowns at work are the result of conflicts stemming from broken execution agreements between individuals or teams.

Execution trust doesn't improve by learning each other's style or gaining conflict management skills, even though these skills are valuable for anyone to learn. This is why focusing on RELATIONSHIPS the way traditional team building tells us to doesn't lead to improved business results. Execution trust improves through establishing clear and shared expectations and agreements, with recovery plans for human error or unexpected disruptions—a greater focus on ENDS, MEANS, and especially COORDINATION.

The only way to achieve high performance is to address two areas that directly impact the achievement of Team Outcomes—improving process and Collective Execution. Even skill building doesn't have a direct relationship to improved performance in the same way that improved processes and Collective Execution do. While most organizations have elaborate programs for improving processes, such as Lean, Six Sigma, and Continuous Improvement programs, they lack any kind of process for improving Collective Execution.

DOING EVERYTHING RIGHT, BUT IT'S NOT ENOUGH

Figure 6 The Missing Piece for Breakthrough Results

To ensure success, every team needs to be focused on achieving Business Results (ENDS). Up until now, the vehicle for making that happen has been to identify and prioritize desired Team Outcomes (MEANS) and optimize Team Relationships (RELATIONSHIPS). But clearly this hasn't been enough for success because it doesn't consider the missing piece (COORDINATION) needed for high performance.

Brian, the CEO of a rural medical center, was exasperated with his organization. They had been working hard the past three years to expand the center's market, lower their costs, and improve their culture. Every month, Brian drove a long list of key metrics and key performance indicators (KPIs) with his extended leadership team, providing development programs to build leadership skills at all levels of the organization, and driving culture initiatives to increase engagement. But the needle hadn't moved, and they were running out of time.

As a rural, full-service healthcare facility, Brian's community depended on their services to prevent traveling two hours to the next nearest medical center. If they had to close their doors, he told me, it would be devastating.

"I get how vital you are to the community," I told him, "but I don't understand why you are in such a critical position to improve."

He told me they'd been operating in the red for two of the last three years and if they weren't profitable by the end of this year, they would be forced to sell to a larger corporation, which would greatly decrease the healthcare services to their community and surrounding area. It was already March; they were currently projecting another loss by the end of the year, and with only nine months left, Brian wasn't sure they could improve their situation fast enough.

I was curious to find out if Brian knew what changes were needed to be successful.

He thought for a moment and was very frank with me, "I'm not sure, but I don't think our leaders understand how critical a situation we are in, so they aren't doing enough to lower our costs and improve our patient care."

As I was pondering his response, Brian continued. "When things don't go well or there is a problem that shows up, I still hear my Executive Team Members and their direct reports blame each other. We can't seem to get on the same page, and it's breaking down our efforts to improve."

Listening to Brian's story, I heard the same frustration I hear with all my clients. Brian was doing everything right according to the advice of all the experts—driving metrics, developing leaders, and engaging employees at all levels. Unfortunately, like so many leaders before him, he was still missing a critical piece of the puzzle for transforming his organization.

TEAM HABITS—THE MISSING PIECE TO IMPROVE COORDINATION

Most people don't remember much from grade school, but they always remember one main idea: Do your own work, get your own good grades, and don't cheat!

MARK SAMUEL

We are trained from an early age to value independence and competition when it comes to accomplishment. Unfortunately, this individualist paradigm doesn't translate well to business. Most people operate based on their comfortable style and their own personal work goals and preferences, *not* what is best to achieve business outcomes to serve the customer and organization. But this would never be how a top-performing sports team, music group, fire department, or military operation would function. High-performing teams start with the outcome in mind and determine the best process, behaviors, and actions to be taken to optimize their results. They do not base their activity on theory or philosophy but on what is practical considering where they want to go, any restrictive conditions they are in, and any possible breakdowns ahead.

It's no wonder businesses have so many competing priorities, conflicts, and breakdowns. They only spend time on aligning processes, not on the execution of those processes, which is where most breakdowns take place. Then, when there is a breakdown, they blame the weakest link, which doesn't help to change the collective Team Habit. Over time, common organizational habits get cemented into place, including the following:

- Silo behavior that doesn't consider the negative impact on other departments
- Decision-making that leaves out others impacted by the decision
- Lack of open information sharing that prevents responsiveness
- Problems that don't get surfaced and resolved due to fear of disclosure

These collective and Team Habits represent an organization's actual culture and method to produce results. If they want to change their results or their culture, they have to change their COORDINATION—their collective Team Habits.

51

THE LEADING METRIC NO ONE IS MEASURING

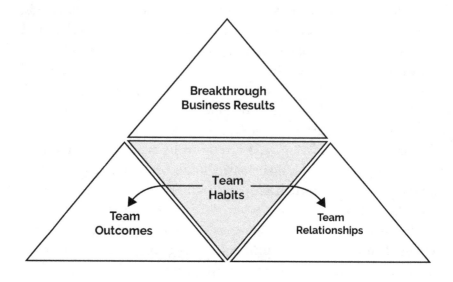

Figure 7 Breakthrough Teams in Action

Team Habits for Collective Execution are the missing piece for achieving breakthrough business results that most team-building programs fail to include. Collective Execution is the way two or more people or groups function together to produce results. Effective Team Habits that the team agrees upon are the linchpin for achieving Team Outcomes and creating positive Team Relationships. Truly high-performing teams like professional sports teams and music groups practice or rehearse Collective Execution because they know that their Collective Execution produces their "leading" metrics, which lead to their "trailing" measurable results. So, while businesses like Brian's medical center are so focused on tracking their leading indicators and KPIs, they aren't even looking at the Collective Execution that drives those results! Their reactions are always going to be late and too slow for significant change.

Let me illustrate the difference in terms of focused time. High-performing teams spend minutes reviewing metrics, some time on their plays or processes, and hours on their Collective Execution to improve their speed and quality of play, communication, decision-making, and recovery when breakdowns occur. Businesses spend hours discussing metrics, some time on processes, and minutes improving Collective Execution—exactly the opposite approach!

Team Habits represent the processes, behaviors, and actions that a team agrees are optimal for producing desired outcomes given the constraints of their organization. For leaders, this includes processes like how decisions are made, how problems are solved, and how information is shared. If you aren't determining as a leadership team the most optimal ways to carry out these essential roles, then it's left to each individual to carry them out in their own ways.

Habits don't change through awareness or skill building. The only way habits change is by replacing an old habit with a new one. We don't even need to analyze the habits that don't work; we know the broken habits by our failed results. Leaders often get caught analyzing failures, but I've found that this most often contributes to divisiveness within a team and doesn't necessarily inform you on how to rethink the processes, commitments, interactions, or follow-up necessary to optimize performance and results. Teams underestimate the degree to which their mindset can get stuck in old paradigms based on a history of silos, autocratic decision-making, or linear handoffs. It often takes letting bygones be bygones and a commitment to focusing on the ideal future to imagine and implement the inclusive cross-functional planning, problem solving, and communication that's required to drive a different model of execution. It's more important to identify what we need to accomplish and determine the ideal processes, behaviors, and actions to achieve the outcome in the optimal way than it is to analyze old behaviors that didn't work.

For an organization, it can't be done individually; it can only be done collectively in the various teams that need to work together in order to achieve common outcomes and business results. Otherwise, you risk unintended consequences for the departments or levels that you didn't include but might very well be impacted.

THERE'S NO OFF-SEASON IN BUSINESS

As I explained this to Brian, he brought up a good point: business teams never have downtime to practice their Team Habits the way that sports teams or music groups do. They operate 24/7 and don't get a break between seasons, games, or performances like other types of teams. But more often than not, business teams don't use their time well, so by shifting *how* they spend their time, they suddenly seem to find plenty of time to practice their Collective Execution!

Leadership teams, department teams, and project teams do actually take some time away from their day-to-day pressures to plan the next year's strategy and goals. So, imagine what would happen if these teams reduced the time they spent on perfecting the plan and spent more time creating and implementing the Team Habits necessary to optimize performance on the plan! Plans are easy to create, but it's in the execution of the plan where breakdowns occur.

I'm sure it comes as no surprise that meetings are the current biggest time wasters in business. Why? Because most meetings are spent sharing information, listening to presentations, reviewing metrics without talking about what will change those metrics, and sometimes even having philosophical discussions and debates that don't lead to any action at all.

The best use of meetings is to access the collective critical thinking that is represented by those in the meeting. This is done by solving problems, making decisions, agreeing on actions to be taken, and aligning on how to share with others to ensure progress of the organization. Meetings are the time to use your team's habits, assess the effectiveness of all Team Habits, and refine them, if necessary, to address different business breakdowns. These kinds of meetings don't only serve the organization due to greater productivity; we have found that these kinds of meetings also increase preparedness, attendance, and engagement among those who attend.

BREAKTHROUGH RESULTS IN SEVEN MONTHS

After completing sessions with the Senior and Middle Management Teams, the medical center in danger of closing produced the following results:

Breakthrough Business Results: Instead of their projected $3M loss, they achieved $3M in profitability. The entire medical center and community got behind their "Save the medical center" message, resulting in a gain from 40% active engagement of employees to 80% active engagement.

Team Outcomes: They defined seven key business outcomes that ranged from financial projects for reducing costs to culture projects for minimizing silo behavior. All seven projects were accomplished on time and on budget. Instead of reviewing all of their metrics, they focused on the game-changing projects with Shared Ownership for removing obstacles that would ensure success. It worked! In addition, many of their stuck metrics also improved, including the following:

- Met eleven out of eleven goals in patient safety and quality metrics that also lowered operational costs. For example, catheter infections dropped from thirty-six to six, and readmissions decreased by 20%.
- When nursing staff leave, a medical center has to hire "traveling nurses," who are very expensive. Their number of traveling nurses dropped from twenty-five to seven in nine months.

TEAM HABITS

The Executive Team created eleven Team Habits. Ten of the eleven Team Habits improved within the first six months. The fifty-five directors on the Middle Management Team agreed to seventeen Team Habits. Eleven of the seventeen Team Habits improved in the same six-month period. That's a lot of new habits that directly impacted communication, performance, and overall culture. Some of the anecdotal comments made by the middle managers about their Collective Execution included the following:

- Meetings are more effective at getting meaningful work done—we focus more on solving problems and making decisions as a team than we do sharing information that we could get in other ways

- Better partnership with the Executive Team and Middle Management Team—now we meet regularly with the Executive Team, and each group holds each other accountable
- Braver about speaking up and sharing ideas openly—managers are much more engaged in our meetings so that we aren't just hearing from the same people from meeting to meeting
- Increased trust between functional areas—now we are feeling more supported by other departments in achieving our department goals. It's amazing how one department reports an accomplishment and owes it all to the support received from one or two other departments
- Increased inclusion of other departments when solving problems and making decisions
- More open-minded about considering new ideas and engaging individual contributors

TEAM RELATIONSHIPS

Team Relationships improved significantly for both the Executive Team and the Middle Management Team, based on the fifteen-question Team Relationship Assessment. The seven-person Executive Team experienced an overall average improvement of 53% on all fifteen areas, including the following:

- Trust improved 76%
- Communication improved 61%
- Managing Conflict improved 56%
- Information Sharing improved 43%

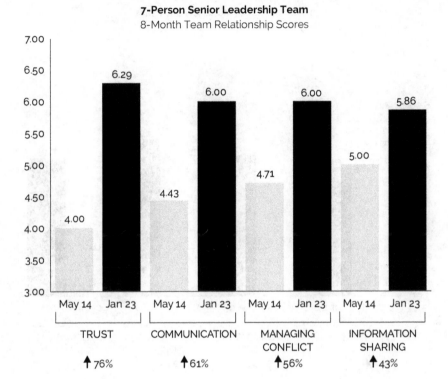

Figure 8 7-Person Executive Team

The fifty-five-person Middle Management Team Relationship Assessment experienced an overall average improvement of 41% for all fifteen areas, including the following:

- Trust improved 41%
- Communication improved 44%
- Managing Conflict improved 52%
- Information Sharing improved 45%

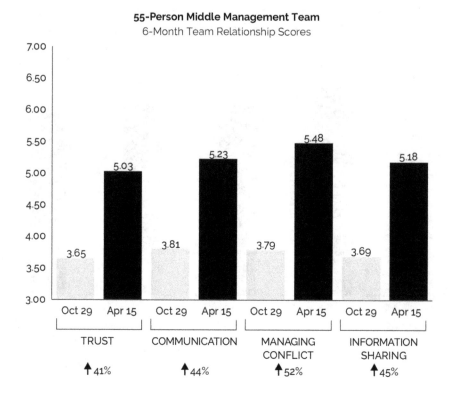

Figure 9 55-Person Middle Management Team

It should be noted that there were no skill-building training programs to improve trust, communication, or managing conflict. This was achieved through their adherence to their Team Habits.

Team Habits aren't a temporary fix. In fact, just like with any sports team or music group, performance generally continues to improve as the members practice their Team Habits together with the clear purpose of achieving better results.

Brian and his medical center continued to run profitably and within three years started to win awards for their accomplishments. They were listed among the top twenty regional medical centers in the United States. They achieved Magnet Excellence and were awarded the Performance Leadership Award. They also were recognized for being among the Best Places to Work in their state.

In the next chapter, you'll learn how to create meaningful and sustainable habit changes that will transform your organization or team. This will include why competencies for establishing high-performing individuals don't create a high-performing organization, and the importance of accounting for mental and emotional changes in addition to behavioral changes for true transformation.

To learn more about how including Team Habits for Collective Execution is the missing piece to team building, you can find the video "Collective Execution" in bstate.com/rt-resources.

5

THE SECRET TO LASTING TRANSFORMATION AND CULTURE CHANGE

"Simple shifts in points of view can open doors to expansion of consciousness."

—Aberjhani

TRUE TRANSFORMATION REQUIRES MENTAL, EMOTIONAL, AND PHYSICAL CHANGE

Even though I was brought up playing sports like baseball, basketball, football, and running cross-country, I always struggled with being overweight. I set weight-reduction goals, modified my eating behaviors, and achieved my weight goal.

We tend to value measurable goals, and physical habits are the easiest ones to measure, compared to mental and emotional habits. So, they get all of our attention. Unfortunately, goals that we can measure on the physical level can be short-lived and thus aren't very effective for sustainable change.

For decades, any time I'd lose weight, it would last for only a month, three months, or up to six months at the most before I began to gain weight again. I learned that achieving goals wasn't very effective as a long-term strategy. I achieved my weight goal many times, only to *un-achieve* my goal within a few months. Changes in behavior habits rarely last, whether it's becoming more organized, exercising, or improving performance at work.

As human beings, we are geared for our personal equilibrium, meaning that our mental, emotional, and physical states all support each other to create our current condition—whether positive or negative. In other words, when I am overweight, my mental state—attitudes, beliefs, mindset about food, self-confidence, and view of what others think of me—are automatically aligned with my emotional reactions to stress, conflicts, or concerns, which are also aligned with my behaviors of eating to calm my stress, prepare for difficult conversations, or soothe my concerns.

While we can use willpower to overcome our mental and emotional responses to stick to a habit change, it's exhausting. Ultimately, we get tired, if not resentful, about denying and controlling, so we give in to the mental and emotional needs that we have been stifling and return to our old behavior.

Lasting transformation takes place only when we are changing our mental, emotional, and physical habits at the same time to support each other in creating a new, higher level of effectiveness for ourselves and in our relationships with others.

THE FAILURE OF FOCUSING ON METRICS

James was a new VP and Site Director for a utility plant in the United States. Ten years earlier, this plant was rated as one of the best in the country—the first quartile as determined by the industry and government's regulatory agencies. The Site Director at the time had very high standards but also led the organization by promoting high-performing, cross-functional teamwork.

Unfortunately, the Site Director had retired nine years earlier and was replaced by a very autocratic leader who led based on control, transforming the plant into silo-oriented departments. At the same time, the corporation that owned the plant decided to turn it into a "cash cow," reaping the profits from its high-performing status, and not investing in maintaining the plant's equipment, developing its people, or keeping up plant operations.

By the time James was hired to run the plant, it was the lowest-performing plant in the country and the only plant in the fourth quartile. While we had been called to help in the recovery effort of other plants in the same industry, this was the first time that we faced the trifecta of major breakdowns—equipment reliability failures from lack of maintenance and upkeep, a broken culture based on poor leadership and siloed departments, and the plant being short-staffed by a whopping 30 to 40%. In fact, the plant had so many unscheduled shutdowns due to equipment failures that it was operating only about 50% of the year! Needless to say, employees were burned out from being overworked, and morale was super low. Even though it was expected to take several years to move the plant back up to the third quartile, if James couldn't get the plant to create enough operational improvement to show an upward trend in operational excellence in the next twelve months, it could be shut down.

In our first meeting, James shared that a breakdown of accountability within their Senior Leadership Team was the reason he had called me for consultation.

"This is bigger than an accountability issue," I suggested. His Senior Leadership Team needed to establish clear expectations so that everyone could be aligned on what they were being held accountable for.

"We have clear expectations," he broke in. "Like all utilities, we have clear metrics that everyone is accountable for achieving."

Unfortunately, metrics only inform you on what needs to be achieved; they don't provide any sense of expectation for what people are accountable for *doing* to achieve those outcomes, which is why emphasizing metrics doesn't help. In James's situation, the team didn't just need action-oriented expectations; they also needed to change people's mindsets and emotional responses to create the high-performing culture James desired.

What most people don't realize is that changing Team Habits can't happen through skill building, establishing new values, or raising awareness. The only way to change a Team Habit is to replace an old habit with a new one that everyone agrees to.

THE DIFFERENCE BETWEEN COMPETENCIES AND TEAM HABITS

You might at this point be wondering, "But Mark, aren't Team Habits just another word for competencies? We already do competencies in our organization. How is this different?"

Competencies are a widely used way to ensure that individuals demonstrate the skills necessary for high performance. They are aimed at *individual* assessment and development. Unfortunately, while individual competencies are critical as a foundation for effective performance, individual competencies don't produce high-performance business results. Why? It's only the effective use of multiple competencies in process with each other that actually produces results.

This is similar to the foundational criteria for hiring and improving individual performance for a sports team or music group. But, as we have all witnessed with sports teams, while each individual needs to have a basic set of individual skills, they win based on team performance and their use of multiple skills in a process—think turning a double play in baseball, a fast break in basketball, or a double-reverse in American football. The same is true in business.

Also, sports teams with star high performers don't always win championships —they are beaten by high-performing teams. The same is true for organizations that have high-performing heroes but fail to grow or meet changing customer demands, because the performance of the organization fails.

An organization I worked with had very clear competencies for their leadership roles, which they used for hiring, evaluation, and professional development. Three of their leadership competencies included the following:

Presentation Skills	Is confident and well prepared when making group presentations. Effectively uses visual aids and handles questions from the audience. Presentations hold the audience's attention with relevant information and are the right length for the amount of information covered.

Problem Solving	Effectively diagnoses the problem, develops a plan to solve the problem, and implements it effectively to achieve results. Recognizes a problem when it occurs, uses logical tools to diagnose it, and then uses rational tools to solve the problem. Asks for help when solving a problem when the problem is outside their area of expertise.
Decision-Making	Investigates all viable options, along with the potential consequences of each, and then makes timely decisions. Can facilitate a group through a decision-making process and does not hesitate to make difficult decisions. Speeds up the decision-making process when a timely decision is necessary.

These competencies describe *what* each leader should be doing but not *how* they need to do it to be effective, especially in a team setting. For instance, the competency for decision-making establishes a criterion for success—investigates all viable options and consequences, makes timely decisions, and facilitates others in making decisions. However, it doesn't articulate "how" to achieve that criterion in context with the role of the leader (executive, middle manager, supervisor) and doesn't include critical aspects for team decision-making that involve communicating the decision, modifying the decision afterward, or evaluating the effectiveness of the decision.

The leadership team in James's organization created a Team Habit for themselves on Cross-Functional Decision-Making that read as follows:

a. We proactively include others impacted by a problem or decision in the problem-solving process and agree on the criteria for making a decision and the method for coming to closure in a timely manner.

b. We anticipate the impact of our decision on the organization's customer, strategy, other departments not directly involved, and employees.

c. We establish a unified communication plan for sharing the decision with others, including the context for the decision, the plan for implementation, and recovery plans for potential breakdowns.

d. We take action consistent with our implementation and communication plans, monitor effectiveness, and modify the decision as necessary, involving the entire leadership team. We don't rehash decisions, and we don't individually make our own modifications without getting approval from the team first.

As you can see from this illustration, Team Habits are customized for the role of the team and integrate multiple competencies to produce a result. In this case, the habit of Cross-Functional Decision-Making included the competencies of Presentation Skills, Problem-Solving Skills, and Decision-Making Skills. While each individual scored high on those specific individual competencies (six out of seven), as a team they collectively only scored two out of seven on effectively performing this Team Habit. As you can imagine, this particular Team Habit on decision-making was the root cause for many breakdowns taking place in the organization, despite the high competency of each individual on the team.

While each individual on the team was highly competent in presentation skills, problem-solving skills, and decision-making skills, they poorly performed the Decision-Making Habit they defined as optimal, because they hadn't been in sync with one another as a team. This is no different from the 2003–2004 Lakers basketball team that had Bryant, O'Neill, Payton, and Malone, four stars of the NBA, but couldn't win the championship because they executed poorly as a team.

RAISING CONSCIOUSNESS—THE FASTEST WAY TO CHANGE MENTAL, EMOTIONAL, AND BEHAVIORAL HABITS

A person's consciousness is the perspective they have that incorporates mindset, emotional responses, and behaviors. As you can imagine, our habits are also highly influenced by our consciousness. As we mature and evolve over time through life experience, we grow from thinking only of ourselves and our own needs and desires to thinking of ourselves within a family, a small community, a nation, and eventually as part of a global community. When we "raise" our consciousness, we view the world from an elevated state of greater wisdom, peace, equanimity, love, respect, joy, intuition, openness, and trust. We can see our effect on the world around us and our world's effect on us, and we can grow out of our small, self-centered view of life to see a bigger picture.

In response to the siloed nature of James's Senior Leadership Team, it was clear that our biggest impact for rapid transformation was to share the Breakthrough State (B STATE) Consciousness Triangle with the team so that they could start to think about the organization as a whole rather than just viewing it from their own self-interest.

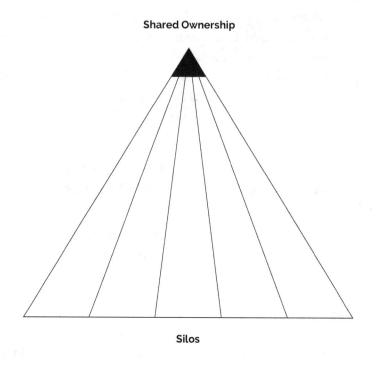

Figure 10   Breakthrough Consciousness Triangle Model

At the bottom of the B STATE Consciousness Triangle pictured above, each leader represents their own particular department. The purpose at the bottom of the triangle is to lead and optimize your department. Within your department, you have your unique priorities that need to be accomplished, and you have your own language of terms that is understood by those in your department. For instance, an immediate problem in Operations means resolve it now by putting your attention on it in the next minute. An immediate problem in Human Resources generally means you can respond to it by the end of day.

As leaders, we tend to make decisions, solve problems, and communicate within the context of our department's priorities and perspective. This siloed approach automatically creates conflicts with other leaders and their departments when they need to rely on each other for information, services, or any other cross-functional need. It's no one's fault. It's just a natural result of being at the bottom of the triangle. When our differences with others result in an impasse at the bottom of the triangle, we either resolve it through a power play in which the most aggressive person with the biggest ego gets their way, through a compromise in a way that both people give up something they need or want in order to appease agreement, or by going to someone higher on the triangle who has greater objectivity and altitude from not being in the conflict. This could be your manager, someone in HR, or an external coach. They may see an alternative solution that those still residing at the bottom of the triangle can't see from their perspective. When we aren't in a dispute at the bottom of the triangle, we have the choice to raise our awareness to a place higher on the triangle to act as mediators for those in the conflict.

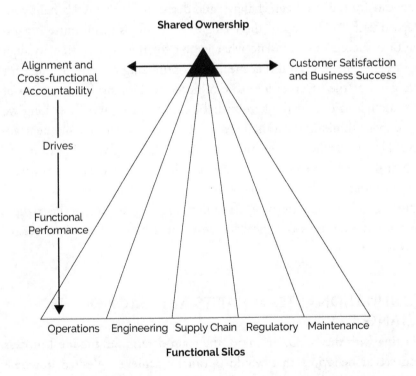

Figure 11 Breakthrough Consciousness Triangle Model with More Details

As you move toward the top of the B STATE Consciousness Triangle, you can no longer see the difference between the different departments, because they all merge together. The top of the triangle represents the services and products of your entire organization. This is the customer's view of your organization. When you reside at the top of the triangle, your purpose is to represent the entire organization in satisfying customers and ensuring organizational viability. You have shared accountability and ownership with the other members of the Senior Leadership Team to surface and resolve any challenge that will impede customer satisfaction or organizational viability, as well as to carry out your individual responsibilities to support team and organizational success.

The role of each Senior Leadership Team member at the top of the triangle is different from your role at the bottom of the triangle. At the bottom of the triangle, your role is to optimize your department and advocate for the resources, changes, and decisions that would benefit your department. At the top of the triangle, your role is to optimize organizational success and translate what is best for the organization to align your department, even if that means suboptimizing your department for the good of the organization. The mindset of thinking from the top of the triangle is one of the hardest habits to change, given how long we have spent thinking from the bottom of the triangle in our silo perspective. However, when we're able to adopt the habit of thinking from the top of the triangle, so many of our bad habits don't make sense anymore and forming new, better habits becomes much easier. When creating and agreeing to Team Habits, the shift to thinking from the top of the triangle in our consciousness is critical for developing habits that are successful and sustainable.

FOUNDATIONAL TEAM HABITS AT THE TOP OF THE TRIANGLE

Starting with the ENDS in mind, the team determines the ideal process and set of behaviors that would optimally achieve a desired outcome based on their actual workplace constraints—not based on current A State standards but on their B STATE desired execution and business results. It's not personality based, style based, or politically based. Additionally, it represents operating at the top of the triangle. It's not philosophical, nor is it a set of goals to be achieved. It's completely behavioral and action-oriented without being so detailed that it becomes robotic or overly restrictive. Team Habits are the closest thing to describing what it would take to "turn a double-play" in baseball or transition from the verse to the chorus to a solo for a rock, jazz, or country band. These are the things that are practiced or rehearsed prior to performing in front of a live audience.

Remember my weight struggles from earlier in the chapter? Even though I was able to change my physical habits for a brief time and reach my goal, this was never a good measure for sustainable success. Inevitably, my old habits resurfaced and I gained the weight back.

When I work with teams on creating new Team Habits, we have to focus on all three kinds of habits—mental, emotional, and behavioral—rather than just focusing on behavioral habit change. Otherwise, the second things get stressful at work, the new habits will go out the window. Below are examples of Team Habits from the mental, emotional, and behavioral realms.

MENTAL TEAM HABIT
We put the organization's needs ahead of our department's needs when prioritizing, problem solving, and making decisions.

EMOTIONAL TEAM HABIT
We respond to breakdowns without blaming others on the team or disengaging when the source of the problem isn't in our area.

BEHAVIORAL TEAM HABIT
We actively support each other in staying at the top of the triangle by speaking up to raise the team's awareness when anyone on the team slips into the bottom of the triangle.

After presenting the model to the leadership team, I met with James in his office. He was excited. "Just using the B STATE Consciousness Triangle will reinforce so many of the changes I have been wanting the leaders to make that they've been unable to stick to," he shared. "They were already referring to the triangle and the new habits as we were discussing organizational issues and changes!"

THE TEAM HABITS AGREED UPON BY JAMES'S SENIOR LEADERSHIP TEAM

The following are three of the fourteen Team Habits that the Senior Leadership Team developed as their priorities for improvement:

1. Being and holding each other accountable for executing core processes

   a. Above all, if a process isn't being followed:
      o We stop.
      o We review the published process.
      o We do it again until we get it right.
   b. We have open communication and collaboration. Barriers are broken down and managers are approachable, providing timely feedback and offering assistance.
   c. We apply self-sustaining processes—new SLT members are supported and quickly included in the team by providing success partners.
   d. Continuous learning and self-assessment for continuous improvement by using Fleet and regulatory feedback is valued and responded to.
   e. We review and assess our processes to identify and resolve breakdowns.

2. Accessible and Responsive Management Team

   a. We proactively schedule time with employees by walking around, listening to their challenges, observing the workplace, and spending time with other departments to surface the biggest obstacles to people getting to achieve their desired outcomes.

b. We ensure effective follow-up and follow through on commitments made to support employees.

c. We provide mentorship for new and existing managers to accelerate onboarding and improved leadership in the plant.

d. Rather than telling managers what to do, we elicit their input, identify and surface holes in their critical thinking, and ask questions to improve their understanding of what to do differently.

e. We ask managers to summarize what they learned and the actions they plan to take to improve results.

3. Make honest commitments rather than just saying yes, and keep those commitments to increase our level of trust, reliability, and consistency

a. We understand what is being asked of us, understand our capacity and capability, evaluate feasibility, and prioritize the request, including saying no if necessary.

b. We properly communicate to those who will perform the action to ensure they have the proficiency and capability to follow through.

c. If necessary, we go to the requestor to negotiate the expectations and competing commitments and priorities in order to adapt expectations based on actual constraints.

d. We regularly update the status on keeping commitments, ask for help if needed, and track our effectiveness in getting closure on open items for completion.

In terms of the Senior Leadership Team's current state, all three chosen Team Habits rated a two out of seven, with seven representing high performance. This is a great indicator that this would represent a true culture change for the Senior Leadership Team, including a new mindset, new emotional responses, and new behaviors.

When the day of creating the Team Habits was completed, James shared his observations: "It was amazing to see the team so quickly develop and align on these new habits of behavior, and while they were creating the Team Habits, they started to behave in accordance with them, even though they were brand new."

"It is amazing, and quite honestly the part I get the most gratification from when implementing this process," I responded, feeling a bit emotional. "When the human spirit is engaged at a higher level of consciousness, it's amazing what people can accomplish together."

When people ask me how long it takes to change a culture, my experience tells me—about one day! This might seem unbelievable, but when people apply a new mindset and a new set of behaviors to produce results, it demonstrates new culture norms. Traditional team building can't do this because it takes the team away from the normal business environment to practice new skills, rather than applying them directly to the job. The key to success and sustainment is making sure that there are follow-up meetings to reinforce the new mindset and behaviors to produce business results from week to week and month to month. Typically, an organization will experience changes in attitude and behavior within a few weeks, see measurable results in three months, and by one year, the new habits, mindset, and behaviors have become the cultural norm!

HOW RAPID SUCCESS LED TO SUSTAINED SUCCESS

About seven months later, we met with James's Senior Leadership Team again to measure results in a blind study that didn't allow them to view their old assessment when developing their current scores.

Even though the Senior Leadership Team had identified only three Team Habits to focus on for improvement (about 21%), they had improved thirteen of their fourteen Team Habits (about 92%) and significantly improved nine Team Habits (about 64%)—a huge difference. More importantly, the regulatory agencies acknowledged the improvement to operational performance, leadership, and culture indicating that they were now ahead of expected improvement results. The plant was saved!

It wasn't a complete win for the plant until they were fully accepted as a second-quartile plant, up from their current fourth-quartile rating. While great improvement in the plant was to be acknowledged, they needed to continue their Team Habits and achieve their goals for improving equipment reliability, hiring hundreds of staff to sufficiently resource the plant, and increasing consistency across the plant in following procedures and achieving results.

During the following year, the plant was rated in the third quartile, which was a huge success. Unfortunately, accompanying that change were two other changes that impacted performance. First, now that they were rated higher, the regulatory agency pulled out the added staff support that it had placed in the plant to help the organization with their recovery. At almost the same time, the pandemic hit while the plant was shut down due to a planned outage to conduct a major overhaul of their equipment. This combination of events caused a ripple effect of challenges for the plant that required people to be on-site instead of being able to work from home. This added several new procedures to keep people safe that resulted in hours of extra time spent by all employees and vendors working on the equipment.

TEAM HABITS ARE ALWAYS EVOLVING

Do you think that the Team Habits of a sports team or music group stay the same once they win the championship or a Grammy? No! Sports teams and music groups are constantly evolving as circumstances change and as the people on the team evolve to higher levels of consciousness and performance.

After the Beatles stopped performing in concert, they changed their habits of playing to become one of the most creative studio bands in the world. Additionally, their Team Habits of recording music evolved when their lives became busier and recording technology advanced to sixty-four tracks up from two tracks, which they were limited to on their first recordings. The impact? In their last few years as a group, they recorded songs separately rather than together in the studio until their very last recording session, when they came back to record together one more time.

James and his Senior Leadership Team created new Team Habits involving taking care of their direct reports and employees in the plant.

James and the Plant Manager created their own new Team Habit in response to the pandemic. They decided to spend 50% of their time speaking with every employee, just to provide a sense of calm, listen to people's challenges, and demonstrate care on a person-to-person level.

Even though the plant went through some challenges, the Senior Leadership and Middle Management Teams adapted very quickly to create a new level of leadership performance on the heels of their embodied existing Team Habits.

In the following chapter, you will experience the power of Shared Ownership and accountability for Team Outcomes that will demonstrate how this misunderstood concept works and is critical for changing culture, improving team performance, and achieving projects in less time and with higher quality.

To learn more about how raising consciousness and thinking cross-functionally can transform your Team Habits and business results, you can find the video "Cross-Functional Teams" at bstate.com/rt-resources.

6

TEAM ACCOUNTABILITY FOR EFFECTIVE CHANGE MANAGEMENT

"Success demands sacrifice, discipline, focus and courage!
Without those, success is fleeting and lucky. With them,
success is sustainable and intentional."

—Michael Nila

THE TRANSITION FROM CONTROL-DRIVEN TO STAKEHOLDER-DRIVEN

Karen, the Vice President of Human Resources for a biotech manufacturing plant, contacted me to discuss an urgent organizational change that needed to be made. They had just replaced their Site VP of fifteen years, who led the plant in a very controlling manner, with a previous member of the team who had been on assignment at their corporate office in Europe. Amir, the new Site VP, was much more participative as a leader, so this was a big change. In addition, they had been acquired the year before and were expected to make major improvements in their plant performance within the next twelve months.

"What are the primary changes Corporate is expecting you to make?" I asked.

Taking a deep breath, Karen responded, "On the business front, we have to improve our safety record, our quality, and our productivity. On the culture front, they don't trust us. When they visit the plant, they experience us as too arrogant and defensive when they surface issues for improvement."

Under a controlling leader who made most of the decisions, the employees didn't develop the level of critical thinking that would foster a "growth" mindset focused on continual improvement and change. So, it's not too surprising that they would feel protective and guarded. I responded and continued with curiosity about their business performance issues. "How large is the plant, and what have you done to improve those areas of performance?"

Karen responded with a bit of frustration in her voice that they had a little over a thousand employees after needing to downsize a couple of years back from about 1,500 people. They reviewed their desired metrics regularly, and it had been a top priority for them to improve their quality and safety for several years, but they hadn't moved the needle on either area. She insisted that everyone was working hard, especially after being downsized, but they were making more excuses than they were real change. "We just don't demonstrate a high level of accountability," she told me. "Everyone is super busy, but we aren't getting better results." With Corporate pressuring them to produce a higher volume of product, Karen was desperate for a change.

Karen's team reminded me of many teams I'd worked with that expect SMART Goals (Specific, Measurable, Achievable, Realistic, and anchored within a Time Frame) to ensure effective execution and results, but still fall short. Like many of my clients, Karen shared, "It's always frustrating to set clear SMART goals, identify change efforts, and still seem stuck in making any significant change."

CREATING A BREAKTHROUGH PICTURE OF SUCCESS

It's clear from Karen's organization history that setting SMART goals for change with metrics to be attained and tracked isn't enough to make a change happen. Every significant change or transformation is an inner-outer process, not an outer-inner process. External goals and metrics don't impact the "inner" changes that organizations, teams, and individuals need to make to embody the change.

A Breakthrough (B STATE) Picture of Success describes WHAT needs to be accomplished *differently* than past results, and it also describes, at a high level, HOW we need to behave *differently* to achieve those results and sustain it afterward.

While it's important to have a general understanding of your Organizational B STATE Picture of Success for setting direction, it's necessary for *each team* to establish their Team B STATE Picture of Success in order to have a clear understanding of what the team needs to accomplish in support of the organization's Picture of Success based on their specific role within the organization. Organizational B STATE Pictures of Success are important, but the most meaningful B STATE Picture of Success is based on the role of the team, because it's teams that need to produce results—Executive Teams, Department Teams, or Project Teams.

If Karen's organization was to impact a significant transformation in their business results and culture to satisfy Corporate's expectations, the Senior Leadership Team had to lead the change—not by telling others what to achieve and do differently, but by how they would lead differently to produce the desired results.

The twelve members of Amir's Strategic Leadership Team (SLT) took about two hours to create and agree on the following B STATE Picture of Success that identified the different behaviors they would need to exhibit in order to lead the organization differently than their historic autocratic approach and that were necessary to achieve their business and culture change.

AMIR'S SLT B STATE PICTURE OF SUCCESS:

As an aligned Strategic Leadership Team (SLT), we are accountable to provide a safe work environment for all employees. We translate business strategy into high standards of organizational execution and behaviors that produce sustainable results. We guide, expect, and empower our managers and their teams to effectively and proactively identify and solve problems to improve the business by utilizing critical thinking skills. We create an open, honest and trusting environment by authentically sharing our own shortfalls with each other, Corporate, and our employees. We provide an environment where systemic fixes are more valued than short-term Band-aids. We've created a safe environment of mutual trust at all levels, financial responsibility, and quick decision-making. We courageously take risks to achieve breakthrough results and learn from our setbacks because we are not afraid to fail.

Within our team we demonstrate and encourage mutual collaboration and supportive accountability for learning and improvement. We support each other and each other's teams by co-mentoring, sharing information and resources, and challenging each other in service of improving our organization. We do what is best for our plant, not our department. We empower our employees, letting go of control, and trusting them to provide the best service for our customers. We provide nonjudgmental and constructive feedback, proactively ask for help, and dedicate ourselves to learning as a role model for all leaders and employees.

As a result, we demonstrate nimbleness, deliver on our commitments, and continuously implement improvements quickly. We consistently drive innovative solutions to achieve a highly safe culture that produces quality products without waste at the lowest possible cost!

When the SLT was asked to rate how well they exhibit the behaviors listed in their Picture of Success, they rated it a two out of seven, meaning that it represented a huge change for them as individuals and as a team.

Their Picture of Success was translated into sixteen Team Habits that described in greater detail the new process and behaviors they would be demonstrating to exhibit the behaviors in their Picture of Success. The process and description of each Team Habit rated one and a half out of seven—an even bigger stretch for the team to comply with. The Team

Habit Titles they focused on improving during the following six months included the following:

1. We effectively translate corporate strategies and goals into a clear direction, strategy, priorities, and expectations for all levels of the plant.
2. We take risks for continuous improvement, learning, and innovation by involving all levels of our organization.
3. We provide a safe work environment and culture of Shared Ownership for achieving a highly safe environment operationally and culturally.
4. We empower employees, let go of control, and trust in one another.

TEAM OUTCOMES THAT DRIVE SHARED OWNERSHIP

When I asked the SLT members to individually identify the plant's top seven organizational priorities, the collective result was thirty-two different "top" priorities, not including the priorities that Corporate gave them throughout the year.

Priorities are misunderstood by most leaders and experts, so it is a moving target that results in confusion, overwhelm, and conflict. Having thirty different "top" priorities like the ones this SLT identified indicates a lack of focus, conflicting priorities, and fragmentation based on which department you represent. Just because your projects are tracked by an internal Project Management Office (PMO) doesn't mean that you're focused enough to move the needle.

There are three different kinds of priorities that all organizations must sort out.

ROUTINE PRIORITIES

Routine (or sometimes called operational) tasks are usually not considered priorities because they involve the things that everyone is doing on a daily basis to serve customers and support the organization to thrive—in other words, they're just what's in people's job descriptions. However, if a routine priority fails to be accomplished, it turns into a crisis that affects either your customer or the health of your business. Therefore, what we do on a routine basis to serve our customers and optimize our business results is always a priority and must be thought of as such.

For instance, I was working with another plant that needed to increase productivity to meet corporate goals, so all of their continuous improvement efforts involved increasing efficiency, effectiveness, and production. However, the following month, they were blindsided by a breach in quality that shut down the plant for three weeks, impacting customers and costing the corporation millions of dollars.

In order to optimize the effectiveness of our routine priorities, we move them to continuous improvement priorities to give them special attention.

CONTINUOUS IMPROVEMENT PRIORITIES

Continuous improvement priorities can be a combination of cross-functional improvement projects generally overseen by the organization or functional projects overseen by the leader of the department. They are generally designed to move from the organization's current state to a better and improved current state—moving from A State to A+ State. There are dozens of improvement projects that can't be managed centrally, so they aren't effectively resourced. One department may need support from another department to accomplish their improvement project. But, in order for the other department to provide that support, they have to allocate resources that weren't planned, which causes a bind. Either they help the other department and divert resources from their own priority project causing a delay, or they ensure their own project proceeds and get blamed for not being a good team player.

Continuous improvement priority projects rarely provide a sense of clear direction for aligned organizational synergy. Ultimately, when a continuous improvement priority project is completed, it goes back to being an improved routine priority. Continuous improvement priorities are critical for staying competitive based on customer demands, industry competition, technological advancements, and shifts in the marketplace.

B STATE PRIORITIES

B STATE priorities are specifically designed for creating breakthrough results. Unlike continuous improvement projects that typically get better in a linear gradual manner based on enhancing processes or skills, B STATE priority projects are aimed at creating a greatly accelerated or huge transformation in the business and in the mindset, process, roles, behavior, and actions across the organization.

Unlike continuous improvement and routine priorities, a team can only handle a maximum of six to eight B STATE priority projects, and many teams choose to only identify four B STATE projects. In fact, it was only a decade or so ago when an organization could handle between eight and ten B STATE priorities, but the increase in routine and continuous improvement priorities has limited the number of B STATE priority projects that can be accomplished.

B STATE priority projects require the following criteria to qualify as breakthrough projects:

1. It is necessary for transforming the business and the culture at the same time.
2. The complexity and scope of B STATE projects require cross-functional problem solving from the team beyond what the project leadership team can do on their own. They include problems involving resource allocation, competing priorities, or decisions that will impact the organization beyond the project itself.
3. It is nonnegotiable for transforming the organization to a new level of business and cultural excellence.

For Amir's Strategic Leadership Team, they chose the following B STATE projects to transform their organization in the next twelve months:

- Safety and Regulatory Compliance
- Upgrading the Quality Control Process and Lab
- Transforming the Role of Middle Managers into an Operational Leadership Team responsible for Plant Operational Excellence and High-Performing Culture

- New Building and Product Ramp-Up
- Building an Authentic and Open Relationship with Corporate Leadership

After agreeing on the top five B STATE priority projects, one of the team members asked a great question: "We identified *safety* as a team habit for improvement and as a B STATE project. What is the difference between the two?"

A B STATE priority project involves setting new expectations, processes, and procedures beyond current standards of excellence. For example, the SLT had to create new expectations and procedures around safety, establishing a speak-up culture in which people at all levels felt comfortable to call out safety challenges. They had to create a Team Habit around how they would role-model safety behaviors and walk the plant to listen and learn from employees on the floor in order to make changes.

Once B STATE priority projects are completed, they become continuous improvement priorities for six months to a year for refinement and then become routine as they're solidified as habits in the new cultural norm.

SHARED OWNERSHIP AND CROSS-FUNCTIONAL ACCOUNTABILITY

You've probably heard the saying, "When everyone on the team owns a project, no one owns it." This is because many leaders and consultants alike don't understand Shared Ownership. I learned about Shared Ownership from playing sports and music. In both situations, if any team member had a problem or made continual mistakes, other team members would come to the aid and assistance of that team member—not to rescue them but to help them build their skills or process to solve the problem. Why? Because we were more dedicated to winning games or having a great performance than we were to doing our minimum part and blaming one another for mistakes.

The way ownership typically works in a leadership team is that one of the team members is assigned to be a sponsor who now "owns" the team project. The sponsor is accountable to their boss for the success of the project. This means that they are expected to solve any and all problems that may arise and take the blame if it doesn't get done. Unfortunately, they aren't in a position to resolve conflicting priorities, resource constraints, or make decisions that will impact the organization beyond the project. This requires the entire Senior Leadership Team. Even the executive in charge of the Senior Leadership Team can't effectively speak for all the areas led by the Senior Leadership Team. Additionally, one of the biggest challenges for a project is the lack of support from areas led by other Senior Leadership Team members because it's not their project to own. Therefore, the sponsor must lead the project while the entire Senior Leadership Team owns the success of the project by removing any organizational obstacles.

For B STATE priority projects, the entire team clarifies a Project Ownership Plan that acts as a more comprehensive Project Charter that includes challenges to successful implementation, cross-functional keys for successful implementation, milestones for tracking progress, and recovery plans for the most common breakdowns that could prevent success. Then, in team meetings, the team sponsor is to surface any challenge or major decision that needs to be addressed by the entire team as a "think tank" to remove any obstacle preventing success.

Ultimately, if a B STATE project fails, the entire team is accountable for the failure.

ORGANIZATIONAL SUCCESS AND TRANSFORMATION IN ONLY NINE MONTHS

Nine months after creating their SLT Picture of Success, Team Habits, and Team Outcomes, we conducted a formal evaluation of their progress to date.

STATISTICAL ANALYSIS

Of the sixteen original Team Habits, thirteen improved. Team Relationships improved an average of 30% in areas such as information sharing, trust, and decision-making.

SLT TEAM MEMBERS SHARE THEIR ACCOMPLISHMENTS

When asking the team members what had changed during the past nine months, they shared that their decisions now prioritize safety and quality over productivity.

"We are doing what is best for the plant instead of what is best for our own departments, which has helped us to create faster alignment on changes," one person wrote.

They also shared that they're communicating with "one voice," addressing challenges, questions, and resistance in a more unified way and are solving more problems in cross-functional groups of two or three instead of in their silos. This speeds up decision-making and increased cooperation during implementation.

CULTURAL CHANGES AND FEEDBACK FROM EMPLOYEES

A climate survey was conducted with all employees, and the results were impressive:

- Leadership demonstrated much improvement in providing clear and aligned direction.
- Organizational fear decreased, while openness to change increased.
- Employees rated Trust in Leadership the highest in over a decade of assessments.

These results were not surprising, given that the SLT ran "Listening Sessions" that responded to issues and concerns expressed by employees. And they created a plant newsletter that shared progress on plant business and improvement goals and acknowledged team and individual successes and contributions.

BUSINESS TRANSFORMATION IMPROVEMENTS AND FEEDBACK FROM CORPORATE LEADERS

One of the biggest changes came from the Operational Leadership Team of about twenty middle managers who led all business initiatives and made operational decisions rather than escalating them to the SLT. From the natural development that took place in that process, there are now seven new middle managers who qualify for promotion to the SLT.

They successfully completed the building of a new Quality Control Lab ahead of schedule, which was a major project for the site. The plant accelerated the timelines for adding new products, demonstrating greater efficiency and productivity. Finally, their previously stuck safety measures improved significantly enough that corporate leaders acknowledged the plant for moving the needle.

Corporate leadership was impressed by the amount of change that took place in such a short period of time. The plant is now a front runner of all thirteen plants in the corporate system and was selected to be the hub for all product testing in the United States. The improvements were not just project completion and business improvements but also represented a new attitude of transparency, ownership of problems, and taking initiative for resolving those issues, fostering a higher level of trust and confidence.

WHEN TEAM HABITS AREN'T ENOUGH TO RESOLVE TEAM RELATIONSHIPS

It's clear from the cases provided that most teams experience significant improvements in Team Relationships based on aligning on and improving their new Team Habits. However, there are times when teams need extra support to address historic breakdowns in teamwork.

There are many different kinds of style inventories that separate diverse approaches in communication, thinking, and working into different groups. This expands people's awareness and openness for communicating with people who are unlike themselves. But, in a changing world that is becoming more diverse and more virtual at the same time, it's critical to develop Team Relationships that go beyond typical group categories. Everyone is unique—we all have different upbringings, environmental circumstances, genetic responses, and belief systems that make us different from any other individual.

Therefore, when improving Team Relationships, developing Team Agreements are critical for allowing each team member to express their own concerns, needs, and desires based on their unique perspective. It is also critical to create a process that adapts to each individual on the team rather than forcing people into an artificial group that overgeneralizes their differences. For instance, introverts tend to be more shy and not speak up, while extroverts tend to do all of the talking. However, this is an oversimplification, and true diversity is more individualistic than simply putting people into categories. These differences must be accounted for to create a truly psychologically safe work environment. Ultimately, people want to be accepted and valued for their individual differences beyond the group they are boxed into that may not fit for them in every situation. This was demonstrated by a twenty-person leadership team I worked with several years ago.

They had low scores in trust, communication, and decision-making. I clearly recognized the problem after observing just one meeting: five people did all the talking while the others remained silent, and everyone was upset about it. The five resented the others for not speaking up, and the others resented the five for dominating every discussion.

They created a guideline for the entire team that read, "Every team member needs to commit to voluntarily share their ideas and opinions on every discussion in our meetings so no one dominates and everyone feels heard."

Everyone on the team agreed to keep to this guideline, except for one person who felt too shy to speak up voluntarily. She wasn't being obstinate; she just didn't want to commit to an agreement she didn't feel she could keep. The team showed up in full support and agreed to make an exception for her as long as she committed to share openly when asked for her opinion or input, which she did.

It's important that teams honor the unique constraints of each individual as long as it doesn't break down teamwork. In this case, because it honored the team member in a way that was mutually agreeable, it actually raised their level of support and trust. The funny thing was that six months later when I came to review the team's effectiveness, the same team member was volunteering her input without hesitation.

I was the one who learned a lesson that day: when people create a truly "safe" environment, they can evolve past their previous labels, styles, and inhibitions to participate with greater courage and confidence. Forming Team Agreements isn't about following the rules; it's about learning how to create a safe environment so that people can evolve to higher levels of trust, support, and transparency.

Once teams align with and implement new Team Habits, demonstrate Shared Ownership for desired Team Outcomes, and demonstrate trust and support in their Team Relationships, they are not only prepared for achieving current desired outcomes, but they also have a team system for continually evolving their effectiveness and approach to the business as they and their business evolve.

7

HARNESSING THE POWER OF TEAMS TO RAPIDLY TRANSFORM YOUR BUSINESS AND CULTURE

"Alone we can do so little; together we can do so much."
—Helen Keller

David was the CEO of a medical center, which had recently made lots of improvements but needed to significantly bring down costs and change their healthcare model to implement a new approach called "Patient-Centered Care."

"To be successful," I told David, "you will need to establish new and expanded roles and expectations at all levels of the organization." This would stimulate the higher levels of personal and team leadership needed to make this transition.

"We have 1,800 employees, not including our physician staff," David responded with concern. He didn't know how they were going to make that kind of change quickly and effectively, especially when they didn't have authority over the physicians who weren't employed by the medical center.

The key to success is leveraging your resources, time, and effort instead of the old mindset of thinking you have to include all employees and physicians to shift the culture. While most organizations and teams make inclusion a goal, this is far too time-consuming to be optimal. Instead of inclusion, the goal should be *representation*, where decision-makers represent the needs, goals, and challenges of others to make an effective decision without unintended consequences to other teams or departments. Until a team or leader has a better understanding of other parts of the business, they need inclusion to ensure representation and avoid unintended breakdowns. However, over time each department's operations, needs, and constraints can be learned, and individuals can make informed decisions that represent multiple areas without having to include those areas because they understand their operations inside and out.

A BUSINESS'S CULTURE IS A DIRECT OUTCOME OF ITS LEADERSHIP ATTITUDES AND BEHAVIORS

If leadership is siloed, then employees at all levels will be siloed, even when they don't want to be. Some exceptions to silo behavior will occur in pockets for improvement efforts, but the way things get done on a daily basis will be siloed.

If executive and middle management don't engage or listen to feedback from their direct reports, then supervisors won't be listening to or advocating for the interests of the individual contributors. If leadership drives performance by pushing people harder without streamlining needless bureaucracy, micromanaging instead of developing their direct reports, or creating a crisis-oriented culture, you can be sure that all employees will be stressed, overwhelmed, and burned out.

"So, we need to fundamentally change leadership if we are to change the organization," David responded. "But we have provided so many leadership training and coaching programs that haven't resulted in significant change. What's missing?"

One of the biggest problems with training programs and coaching efforts is that they are designed to be *individual-oriented*. They don't provide any training on practical teamwork. In other words, there's no *collective* accountability.

"My Executive Leadership Team is pretty far removed from daily operations," said David. "So how will changing them make the biggest difference?"

Often, the Executive Leadership Team can be the change catalysts, setting the direction for change. But more often than not, it'll be a *united* team of middle managers who become the change agents for driving the business and the culture.

In most organizational structures, the middle managers are only accountable for their department results, not what is good for the entire organization. As a result, they are experts on the "technical" functioning of their department but don't understand the impact of their decisions on the business or the unintended consequences that negatively impact other departments. The only way middle managers become effective is when they are unified into a team with a common purpose greater than their department and with accountability to each other.

We have been sold on the idea that change is either top-down or bottom-up, and there are many methodologies that attempt either approach. Unfortunately, top-down change never gets to the lowest levels of an organization, usually getting stuck at middle management, and bottom-up change never goes up to leadership effectively, leaving out middle management and failing to address cross-functional organizational systems that are dysfunctional.

Because both top-down and bottom-up change get stuck at middle management, they are often viewed as the weak link. But in reality, a unified and accountable middle management team is the key to success.

THE MISSING TEAM IN ORGANIZATIONS

Executives or senior leaders have a sense of belonging as part of a leadership team. Individual contributors belong to a group identity known as non-managers, especially if they are unionized. The only group within an organization that doesn't have a group identity is middle managers. They don't meet as a team, even though they may attend a larger extended leadership team meeting that is led by senior managers. The problem? They have no accountability to each other; they're only accountable to the senior manager to whom they report. This is how silos and an "us versus them" mentality gets activated, causing performance failures and a "blame-game" culture.

The "divide and conquer" approach to getting things done sounds effective, but *only if* those divided are already aligned and supporting each other. When senior leaders identify priorities and projects that are delegated to different upper middle managers, it naturally results in competing priorities and a lack of support among the departments led by those middle managers.

By creating a unified team of upper middle managers, their role automatically expands to the purposes that unite them: optimizing operational excellence and creating a healthy culture. As a team, upper middle managers representing all parts of the organization ensure that cross-functional priority projects, processes, and workflows are optimized through effective planning and coordination as needed. They also address any breakdowns in the culture by establishing clear expectations, building trust between departments, and engaging other levels of management and individual contributors in a consistent way across all departments. Why? Because now they are not only accountable to their senior leader, but also to each other for supporting team decisions, expectations, and commitments.

In David's medical center, the department directors formed the Operational Leadership Team (OLT) in charge of organizational change, operational excellence, and culture. While the Executive Leadership Team (ELT) developed the Strategic Plan and set business priorities, the OLT led cross-functional execution. They prioritized projects and made decisions with an accountability for achieving the desired outcomes set by senior leadership.

At first, the OLT was fairly dysfunctional. They didn't understand how to best work as a team, since they were only developed to be individually effective for their own department. They lacked the necessary skills for being part of a leadership team and had difficulty relating to the ELT in a healthy manner that wasn't either too independent or too attached to pleasing the ELT. In some ways, it reminded me of dealing with teenagers who are looking for independence but still expecting parents to provide for them.

To coach the OLT members through this challenge, I met with them and shared that in their new role as a team, they would need to gain influence and build trust in their leadership *as a team*, especially with the ELT.

I provided the following choice of behaviors that they could exhibit to either increase or decrease trust with the ELT:

LOSING INFLUENCE & TRUST WITH THE ELT	GAINING INFLUENCE & TRUST WITH THE ELT
• Negatively judge ELT and look for evidence to criticize them	• Look for ways to acknowledge the ELT's good ideas, decisions, or behaviors, or for including you in their process
• Individually critique ELT proposals, plans, or suggestions (positive feedback *can* be given individually)	• Strategize, plan, and provide constructive feedback as a unified team with "one voice" (even if you need time to prepare)
• Look for permission from or wait for ELT input to make recommendations for change, priorities, or solutions	• Take initiative by strategizing and making recommendations to the ELT in a way that is open to receiving their feedback, learning, and adjusting your proposal based on discussion

• Act as know-it-all experts by resisting feedback or suggestions from others—ELT, direct reports, or coaches	• Act as students/learners by asking questions to gain understanding, raising concerns with *openness* to other's input, and demonstrating humility
• Share OLT discussions with ELT members without permission from the OLT as a team, creating fragmentation or distrust with your other OLT team members	• Keep confidentiality and accurately represent the OLT when communicating to others as a unified voice
• Loudly speak your opinion or idea in a way that dominates discussion or discourages input from others	• Share your opinion openly, and facilitate others on the team to share their opinions or ideas to promote diverse critical thinking and perspectives
• Propose recommendations that are emotionally based or data based, which lead to faulty conclusions due to a lack of context	• Propose recommendations that are evidence based using a "pilot study" or a business case that integrates human factors and data analysis, and uses case studies

Seeing the choices laid out made an impact that led to their rapid success. Within six months, decisions were being made faster and with more of an operational perspective from the OLT rather than being escalated to and solved by the ELT, which took much more time and didn't consider challenges to operational implementation. By the end of the year, the OLT successfully accomplished more priority projects set by the ELT than in any previous year, lowered operating costs, and broke down most of the silo behavior between departments at all levels, representing a huge change in their business and culture. But the transformation didn't end there.

HIGH-PERFORMING DEPARTMENTAL TEAMS

During the second year, in addition to having even more and larger priority projects delegated by the ELT to the OLT, the OLT wanted to extend the team process to the rest of their departments. With the support of certified trainers from their organization, every department created their own Picture of Success, Team Habits, Improvement Plans, and Team Relationship Agreements. This engaged all employees in the process of creating their optimal future in terms of streamlining and improving procedures as well as increasing support within each team. They all included Team Habits that would optimize their relationship with other departments in addition to supporting physicians and patients. Each department posted their departmental Picture of Success and Team Habits at the entryway of their department to inform others of their commitment to support teamwork. This created a higher level of positive accountability in terms of responsiveness, communication, and follow-through.

By the end of the second year, David's medical center was winning awards for quality, low patient stays in the medical center, employee satisfaction, and patient experience. There was a vibe when you walked the halls between employees of all levels acknowledging each other for successes, asking questions, and asking to meet with others in different departments to discuss a challenge or coordinate a new project. Even the medical center cafeteria improved so much in ambiance and food quality that people in the community would come there to eat, even if they weren't visiting anyone in the hospital. That's something you don't hear every day about hospital food!

While members of the ELT and OLT were invited to speak at health-care conferences to share their process for changing their culture and business results in such a short time, the organization established a new revenue stream by hosting paid education sessions for medical center administrators from around the United States to learn how they had established their culture of patient-centered care, healing healthcare, and accountability. They typically had forty to fifty participants per quarter taking part in their culture change education program.

SUSTAINING A TEAM CULTURE: HIRING, ONBOARDING, PERFORMANCE MANAGEMENT, AND SUCCESSION PLANNING

Each team evaluated their Team Habits, accomplishment of Team Outcomes, and their Team Relationships every six months for the first two years to continue their focus and measurement on improvement and expansion, and once a year afterward for ongoing improvement and sustainment.

However, the OLT leaders wanted to solidify their team culture even more by structuring teamwork into the fabric of their organization. The OLT developed an organization-wide project to rewrite their job descriptions to emphasize outcomes and expectations of each role and the cultural norms established by each department's Team Habits. They also used the department's Team Habits in the interview process for hiring new employees to ensure that they would bring people into the organization who were excited and committed to the culture and standards of high performance. This was repeated during the onboarding process, and team members were used to orient new team members into their team based on sharing their experience and documentation from the Team Session that developed Team Outcomes, Team Habits, and Team Relationships.

Then each OLT leader redesigned their Performance Management forms by replacing the competencies previously used with the Team Habits that their team developed. It was expected that each individual's performance score would be equal to or better than the level of team performance for each Team Habit. This provided much more meaning to their individual performance assessment, was instructional for weaker areas of an individual's performance of a Team Habit, and provided a way for team members to mentor each other—similar to how athletic teams or music groups operate.

These systems established complete consistency and integration of hiring, onboarding, individual performance, team performance, and succession planning for all levels of the organization. More importantly, these systems were driven by input from all employees in their departments when they developed their Picture of Success, Team Habits, and Team Relationship Agreements. Everyone was excited to have a personal stamp on the direction of their department, the high performance desired and attained, and a culture that was mutually trusting and supportive.

THE POWER AND SPEED OF CROSS-FUNCTIONAL ACCOUNTABILITY AS A TEAM

Another shift that took place during the third year elevated the organization to another level of high performance. By now, each middle manager on the OLT had a very good understanding of all other departments—not technically, but from a leadership perspective of understanding priorities, constraints, strengths, and weaknesses of the departments within the organization. This allowed for a new level of speed for making decisions. By now, each OLT member was a witness to the evolution of gaining speed for solving problems and making decisions:

STAGE	DESCRIPTION	SPEED AND EFFECTIVENESS OF DECISION-MAKING
1	Before middle managers became a team	Silo decision-making was fast but resulted in breakdowns during implementation, causing wasted time, money, and effort.
2	Decision-making as an OLT or subset of OLT members	Collaborative decision-making took more time, but implementation was much faster and smoother with fewer breakdowns costing wasted time, money, and effort (projects were completed on time and on budget).
3	Decision-making by OLT members without needing input from other OLT members	OLT members were so knowledgeable about each other's departments, many decisions could be made by individual OLT members, but with full cross-functional consideration and trust between department leaders, resulting in accomplishing three times the number and magnitude of organizational projects.

Judy, the director of the laboratory, created a business case study for significantly increasing revenue and profitability by doubling the size of the laboratory to be even more competitive in their region. It was a great plan and was approved by the ELT. However, it needed approval by the OLT for effective implementation as part of their role overseeing Operational Excellence and Culture.

When Judy presented her proposal to the OLT, the other OLT members were in unanimous agreement that they *would not approve* Judy's plan to double the size of the laboratory.

Judy was shocked and asked her team why, especially since it was already approved by the ELT.

One of the OLT members spoke for the team, "Because the culture of your department is not healthy and you are sitting with five grievances from individual contributors and three pending lawsuits from disgruntled employees in your department. We are not in favor of doubling the size of your department until the culture within your department is improved."

"I understand your concerns," Judy rebutted, "but this is a huge financial opportunity that the medical center needs for increasing profitability and viability."

Another OLT member spoke up, "That's why we are going to have two OLT members who are very strong at building morale and enhancing the culture be your personal coaches and consultants to set up the systems and practices to improve the culture in the lab."

"Our goal would be to have your department cleared of grievances and have an increase in morale within six months," another OLT member spoke up. "We aren't going to risk more lawsuits so that you can expand— it just isn't fiscally or culturally responsible."

While disappointed, Judy agreed to receive the support, and this became an OLT project that was tracked at each of their OLT meetings.

Five months later, the department's culture was cleared of grievances, morale improved significantly, and Judy was super pleased by the coaching and support she received. The OLT approved the plan for doubling the lab, and before the end of the year, the new part of the lab was set up and implemented, with the full support of all of the departments connected to the lab's growth.

A BENCHMARK IN THE HEALTHCARE INDUSTRY FOR TWELVE YEARS

For twelve years, David's medical center achieved accolades for their continued benchmark scores leading the industry in quality, patient satisfaction, patient length of stay, employee satisfaction, and financial profitability. The medical center was the first to receive a five-star rating from the U.S. government for their energy efficiency and was one of the first innovators of menu service to patients. They were highly rated as a role model by the Joint Commission on Accreditation of Healthcare Organizations (JCAHO), now referred to as the Joint Commission. They were also one of the first medical centers to be ISO-certified. They continued to achieve several awards maintaining their benchmark status. David continued to be asked to present at leading healthcare conferences until he retired after twelve years of sustained success by his medical center.

In the next chapter, you'll learn the core team competencies that are often ignored but are key for driving active change and business transformation.

8

THREE TEAM CORE COMPETENCIES NO ONE TEACHES

"Momentum really is the most important aspect of deliberate creation that you could consciously contemplate. Because what momentum says is: Once you get going in that direction, it is more likely that you will continue in that direction."

—Abraham-Hicks

In general, it's easy to set goals, metrics, and desired results. It's relatively easy to create a plan based on those goals. Why is it so easy? Because there is no real way to fail until you take an action on the plan and start to move toward the goals that you set. We have all had the negative experience of taking action on a plan that resulted in mistakes or even failure that was then criticized by others. We may even have felt branded by the experience, carrying with us a blemish that impacts us for years.

To make matters worse, if the goals and plans were done with a high level of due diligence and it fails during implementation, it's not the planners who get blamed; it's the implementers! Putting blame on those who take action creates a culture void of forgiveness, which is required for learning, and perpetuates a cycle of fear, causing hesitancy and reluctance to move, let alone try new things or take risks. It's no wonder we avoid taking action on our goals. But it's only through action that we can possibly achieve success.

Taking action and being accountable for results strikes fear in many of us—it's just too risky. To ease our fear, we spend time deliberating over the analysis we put into setting the right goals and metrics or into refining and perfecting the plan and making sure we get the buy-in from everyone involved to ensure success. As we'll see in the next example, overanalyzing and over-perfecting often leads to additional breakdowns.

TWO APPROACHES TO CHANGE MANAGEMENT

PPSA was a Latin American petroleum company implementing a major corporate restructuring and introduction of new technology that would change the process of production. This improvement effort would affect all of their four major divisions. While the change effort was the same, each division was given permission to use its own approach for implementing the change. Two divisions were located near each other, so their different approaches were visible to each other.

M Division used a more traditional approach to change management by hiring a large international consulting firm to lead a strategy that engaged about 60% of the workforce in a bottom-up approach to planning and implementing the change. Senior management provided a clear direction and expectations, while multiple cross-functional task forces were created that included a combination of middle management and individual contributors to tackle different aspects of the organizational change in a "divide and conquer" approach.

Each task force had three months to develop a plan for implementing change that would be reviewed by a change management group and the external consultants leading the change. One of the goals for this approach was to empower, increase employee engagement, and create universal buy-in from all levels of the division to optimize implementation of the change. Based on the excitement and enthusiasm that everyone shared during the first couple of months, it was on track for being highly successful.

With my help, L Division used a B STATE (Breakthrough State) team-based approach to managing the change. While the role of senior management was similar in providing a clear direction and expectations for the change, senior and middle management were brought together as an expanded leadership team that developed a clear Picture of Success for what the organization would need to look like after the change. They put special focus on how they would need to operate as a unified team with Shared Ownership and cross-functional, cross-discipline accountability to implement the change.

The expanded leadership team then identified key change agent leaders at every level of their respective organizations to be part of an expanded set of teams that would plan and drive the change. While M Division included about 60% of their employees, L Division included only about 15% of its organization in planning and leading the change from a mostly top-down approach. Instead of M Division's approach to take the time and involve a mass number of people to develop a "close-to-perfect and widely accepted" plan for implementation, L Division's approach was to produce a plan and begin implementing it within four months with a focus on Proactive Recovery Plans to course-correct as the plan was being implemented.

SPEED AND SIMPLICITY BEAT OVER-PLANNING AND COMPLICATION

By the third month of implementation, M Division began seeing break-downs in its change management approach. As task forces were presenting their plans, it became clear that their approaches to implementing change were in conflict with each other. As a result, the next three months were dedicated to sorting out their differences and developing a unified strategy for moving forward.

Unfortunately, this was harder to achieve and resulted in several conflicts that became more and more polarized over time. In addition, it created a level of confusion and lack of confidence among the task forces. It took an additional three months (nine months after starting the project) to finally begin implementation, but now instead of people feeling empowered and excited by being included in the change effort, people were frustrated by the challenges and confusion between task forces resulting in even greater skepticism and resistance. Leadership decided to postpone the change effort another two months to diminish the negativity that arose.

Using their B STATE Picture of Success, the L Division's Expanded Leadership Team didn't start by planning the change effort. They began by identifying all the functional and cross-functional/discipline areas that were not operating consistently with the new B STATE Picture of Success approach to execution. In other words, they developed Team Habits and Relationship Agreements for cross-functional problem solving and decision-making, transparent information sharing, and engaging employees at all levels. It took about three weeks to have agreed-upon commitments for optimal team functioning to replace old silos and conflicting behaviors. The agreed-upon Team Habits and Relationship Agreements were monitored for effective implementation.

Once that was completed, the Expanded Leadership Team led change management planning sessions with their multi-level change agents according to the Team Habits and Relationship Agreements established by cross-functional teams. Where they couldn't agree, the cross-functional teams developed Proactive Recovery Plans to address any challenges or breakdowns that might occur during actual implementation of change. With full alignment, the Expanded Leadership Team, together with the multilevel change agents, communicated the change at different levels of the organization with the multilevel change agents being the primary influencers of the 85% of the employees not directly involved in the change.

As a result, implementation began only four months after the initiation of the change project. By the eighth month, the implementation of change was completed, and by the twelfth month, they achieved their highest petroleum productivity goals in five years while meeting their cost-saving goals and improving morale to become the new benchmark for the corporation with the highest scores in performance and employee satisfaction.

In summary, instead of going for inclusion and full organizational buy-in like M Division did, L Division focused on the new culture of execution and leveraged a few change leaders to provide clarity for the change that was easily adopted by the rest of the organization. Why did this work? Because the cross-functional Expanded Leadership Team provided a clear road map for success, removed opportunities for blame by accounting for potential breakdowns, and placed their focus on the desired outcome for the business and culture that kept everyone focused on the big picture rather than any negative judgment about the details of change that naturally need to be adjusted along the way.

CORE COMPETENCY #1: TAKING IMPERFECT ACTION TO DRIVE MOMENTUM

We have all seen a 100-meter dash. The sprinters start out with their feet positioned on the blocks and hands on the track in preparation. Upon hearing the starting gun, the sprinters are required to exert the greatest amount of energy, effort, and focused drive just to take the first three steps. After that, movement and momentum will help them out.

The same is true in organizations. The first actions to implement a new change effort require a lot of energy to overcome resistance, the learning curve, competing priorities, and the discomfort of doing things differently. Those initial actions are difficult, and it's easy to get discouraged, frustrated, and skeptical when they don't go as smoothly as you would like. This can cause us to give up, revert back to our old ways of doing things, or get distracted by other priorities or challenges. Of course, anyone who wasn't in favor of the change can easily use this initial hiccup as justification to negate the change. If the change needs to be made for the sake of the business, the process starts again, but this time with even more skepticism, resistance, or hesitation from those involved. Who wants to invest their time and energy in something that will get reversed when the going gets tough? This is what I call the Action Phase of Change.

Once the sprinters make the grueling effort to take their first three steps at the start of the race, they develop a rhythm and flow that requires less effort for continual movement. It generally takes anywhere from three to six months of an organizational change to move into the rhythm and flow that goes into the Movement Phase of Change. In this phase, people are more focused on solving problems and moving forward than using it as an excuse for stopping the effort or going back to the way things used to be.

As the sprinters reach about 50% to 75% of completion, they enter their full stride. They go from the flow of the Movement Phase to the Momentum Phase, where it's not just the energy they are putting into their stride that's moving them forward; they are compelled by an extra force. How can you tell? They can't quickly stop! In fact, the inertia of forward motion is so strong it would cause harm if they were to immediately come to a stop. That's why we see runners cross the finish line and generally keep running to slow down before they stop.

The same is true for change efforts in an organization. Once the organization takes consistent action with the flow of continuous movement, they enter the Momentum Phase of Change, which makes it hard to stop and ultimately becomes the new culture of the organization. This can take anywhere from about nine months to two years, based on the complexity and size of the change.

The key to success of any large change effort in an organization is to take action, keep moving through the difficult learning curve, adapt based on the lessons of experience that no one can know prior to the change, and continue to move with clear focus until a critical mass of movement is generated to create momentum.

CORE COMPETENCY #2: PROACTIVE RECOVERY TO DRIVE COOPERATION AND SPEED

What do the highest-performing sports teams, music groups, theater groups, and dance companies have in common? They all recognize that great performances don't depend on perfection. They recognize that as human beings, even the highest performers in the world still make mistakes, miscommunicate, and don't keep all of their commitments.

Given the nature of human experience, top-performing teams create and practice Proactive Recovery Plans instead of hoping and planning on perfect performance. They don't call them Proactive Recovery Plans, but they make sure to practice those circumstances that are the most vulnerable to breakdown. This includes a team member missing the ball or a tackle, a musician's string that breaks during a live performance, an actor who forgets lines, a malfunctioning prop or set piece, or a dancer who misses a step.

While effective organizations and project teams create risk-mitigation plans or contingency plans in anticipation of equipment breakdowns, utility breakdowns, and unpredictable circumstances, they don't generally create recovery plans for human error.

A medical center that created Proactive Recovery Plans for over three years had to move two nursing units from the second floor to the fourth floor of the medical center to improve efficiency and reduce operating costs. Both nursing unit management teams involved their staff and other functional areas to coordinate the transition to the upper floor.

After the transition to the new floor, one nursing unit's move was completely successful, with no interruption in patient care. The other nursing unit didn't function well at all. It didn't work for patients and didn't work for nursing staff. The cross-functional Proactive Recovery Plan that was used to remedy the situation involved a ten-step process of getting approval multiple times from the executive team and moving the beds back and forth from the second floor to the fourth floor.

When I asked medical center leaders how long they thought the time frame was to move back and forth from the second to the fourth floor, the response was between six and twelve months to accomplish all ten steps. The actual time was less than thirty days—at least six times faster than it would have been if they hadn't used the core competency of Proactive Recovery Plans.

KEY COMPONENTS OF A PROACTIVE RECOVERY PLAN

1. Take the time with cross-functional and multilevel stakeholders to identify potential breakdowns and develop an aligned way to mobilize the necessary resources to make new plans and decisions quickly and effectively.
2. Demonstrate the highest levels of respect, cooperation, and support without any wasted time blaming anyone or any department for breakdowns.
3. Establish ownership and accountability in all levels of the organization for optimal performance and customer service.

CORE COMPETENCY #3: SHARED OWNERSHIP FOR OUTCOME-DRIVEN MEETINGS

In most organizations, the responsibility for the meeting is with the meeting leader, which means others show up as observers rather than active participants or co-leaders. These information-sharing sessions that focus on updates, presentations, or metrics rarely add much value, leaving people feeling like their time has been wasted.

One of the keys for successful meetings is that members of the meeting take ownership for its success in addition to the leader who organizes the meeting. This requires that each meeting is clear about the value-added desired outcomes for the meeting and that all participants help to keep it focused on achieving those desired outcomes.

Ellen, a project leader with twelve people on her project management team, was charted to build and open a new facility with the latest high-end chemical manufacturing equipment. During our introductory meeting, Ellen was weary from working six twelve- to fourteen-hour days per week, trying to get her project back on schedule.

"I'm not sure you can help us," she complained. "I've been assigned project managers who overpromise and under-deliver. We have two external vendors who have their own ways of doing things and blame us for not achieving their deliverables. And the plant's leaders are constantly upset with the design of the building that optimizes the new equipment but doesn't look like the configuration of the current building with their antiquated equipment."

"How are you tracking progress on the project?" I asked.

Ellen responded with confidence, "We have regular meetings with the project management team that includes our vendors, and we review all of the commitments, schedules, and necessary changes we have to make due to broken commitments and missed due dates." She told me about the in-depth presentations, explaining the actions taken to accomplish deliverables, and was proud to announce that every team member participated in the meetings, though she also admitted some got distracted with handling more pressing issues.

Many leaders like Ellen think their meetings are outcome-driven because they review deliverables and schedules, but in reality these are just status update meetings. Meetings that are too focused on status updates and information sharing are one of the top reasons teams don't achieve their desired outcomes on schedule. Teams must meet to focus on the desired outcome of removing obstacles to success that all project managers on the team have ownership for resolving.

Once per week, the project managers and vendor managers who Ellen was working with met to surface any anticipated breakdowns that might take place within the next one to three months if not resolved. Then the entire project management team offered and discussed possible ways to prevent the surfaced breakdowns. The project managers directly involved decided on a course of action with timing for sharing results back to the team. The purpose of these meetings was not tracking results as much as it was solving problems, making decisions, and taking action.

In about three weeks, the project management team learned that in many cases, those not directly involved were the ones who had the most creative suggestions for resolving breakdowns. Also, participation increased significantly in these meetings, as did accountability for taking action on recommended solutions. Within six weeks, the number of crisis management situations was diminishing, project managers were collaborating more to resolve breakdowns outside of these meetings, and deliverables were meeting schedule expectations.

TEAM CORE COMPETENCIES IN PLAY

While organizations and teams have various levels of success, over time we have noticed that the most successful organizations and teams demonstrate all three core competencies. It was their ability to focus on aligned action, not perfect action, that created the necessary movement and momentum to deliver results faster than they had thought possible. It was their Proactive Recovery Plans that enabled them to move from a culture of blame to one where people take initiative, take calculated risks, and support one another through the ups and downs of change requiring the highest levels of resiliency. And it was through their meeting structure, which emphasized Shared Ownership for anticipating and solving breakdowns proactively, that enhanced critical thinking, improved decision-making, and resulted in higher-quality output and better customer experience.

In the next chapter, you'll learn about how to address some common team quandaries as well as how to apply the rest of the book to different kinds of teams that exist in organizations, including leadership teams, department teams, project teams, and self-managed teams.

To learn more about successful change management, you can find the video "The Key to Successful Change Management Is Movement" at bstate.com/rt-resources.

9

TAKING YOUR TEAMS TO THE NEXT LEVEL

"Permanent excellence is an illusion; you have to keep regenerating your portfolio."

—Renée Mauborgne

Sports teams, music groups, and business teams cannot afford to rest on the laurels of their success from having high-performing Team Habits and solid Team Relationships that produce breakthrough results. Competition, customers, the economy, and environmental conditions are constantly changing and demanding new levels of team effectiveness and results.

One such change happened recently and challenged teams of all types, levels, and industries. It even changed the game of team building itself. In 2020, when COVID-19 became a worldwide challenge, many organizations were at risk of going out of business. Teams could no longer meet in person, and all off-site team building was canceled. This forced teams everywhere into a virtual space that was unfamiliar for many.

VIRTUAL TEAM BUILDING—MAKING THE IMPOSSIBLE A REALITY

Today, more than any other time in history, teams comprise of people who reside in different cities, states, and countries. Yet the need for effective planning, coordination, communication, and problem solving is as critical as ever. Getting together in the same physical space for team meetings has become impossible for some organizations, and even getting teams together for an in-person team-building retreat can be time consuming, costly, and impractical. During the pandemic of 2020–21, teams could no longer rely on regularly socializing together, going out to dinner or concerts together, or enjoying a company party to build trust and a feeling of support for one another. During that time, teams were forced to connect, pivot, plan, and even resolve issues within the team virtually, and we learned a lot.

HEALING BROKEN TRUST, LOW PERFORMANCE, AND LOW MORALE IN A VIRTUAL SESSION

A government and union-based organization in Canada had a huge breakdown in trust. The situation was so bad that some team members, including leadership, were out on leave due to the resulting stress and health challenges. Because of restrictions due to COVID, there was no way to get everyone in the same room at the same time to build trust and support, even though the trust was so broken.

We were able to lead the team in developing their B STATE Picture of Success as well as Team Habits to support effective execution, teamwork, trust, and support. The team felt so strongly about their new Team Habits that they signed their Team Habit document to demonstrate their commitment to each other and to ensure that any newly onboarded members would also support the culture they were creating. Their new Team Habits clearly described how they were going to share transparently with individual contributors and include them in decision-making that involved their roles and responsibilities.

Not only did each supervisor and the department leader have a new sense of commitment to each other and clear expectations for effective performance, trust, and support, but they also had a way to include every employee in a united dedication to their individual contributors and service to the community. In only six weeks, individual contributors were volunteering to cover for each other when anyone was out sick or they were short-staffed. They were volunteering for task forces to improve operations and teamwork. Morale quickly went up, as did performance and cross-training in an effort to support the development of each person on the team.

They still couldn't socialize with each other, but it didn't keep them from demonstrating a high level of trust, support, cooperation, and commitment to each other.

MERGING TWO TEAMS WITH OPPOSITE CULTURES AND "US VS. THEM" BEHAVIOR

In a different scenario, a high-tech company recently acquired a company with a very different culture. This created an "us vs. them" mentality and behavior that was tearing down the teamwork that had existed before. Even though both cultures were different, each had positive attributes. One company was very results-driven, decisive, and accountable, but not very team-oriented. The other company was very team-oriented but took a long time to make decisions and drive change.

The leaders on the team lived in different parts of the U.S., and it was too expensive and time-consuming to bring them all together for a team-building session. Instead, they ran a virtual program in which they created a B STATE Picture of Success, taking the best of both cultures. Their Picture of Success described a new culture that integrated a results-driven, decisive, and accountable culture with a high level of team planning, coordination, and cross-functional problem solving.

Everyone left the experience energized, feeling complete identity with their new leadership team and culture that they themselves architected to optimize their performance and relationships.

There has been no difference in quality outcomes between building a team virtually or in person. Even when people don't know each other very well or come from different cultural experiences, or when there is a history of broken trust at the deepest levels, virtual sessions based on aligning on Team Outcomes, Habits, and Relationships have proved highly successful!

APPLYING THE MISSING PIECE TO DIFFERENT BUSINESS TEAMS

BUILDING EXECUTIVE AND SENIOR LEADERSHIP TEAMS

Executive and Senior Leadership Teams have five primary responsibilities that can only be achieved by their level of leadership.

1. They must identify the external drivers that will either threaten their organization or provide unique opportunities that must be leveraged.
2. They must develop creative ways to direct the organization's highest priorities for business results and changes in high-level execution that will set the organization up for success.
3. They must translate those desired outcomes into clear high-level priorities that leverage the organization's resources to achieve break-through results.
4. They must allow their Middle Management Team to create operational plans that will achieve those highest-level priorities and shift the culture in a way to support those largest initiatives.
5. They must remove the obstacles that prevent the Middle Management Team and individual contributors from being successful. This includes addressing conflicting priorities to provide clear direction, adding or redistributing resources as necessary for achieving the highest-level initiatives, and making decisions that will impact multiple high-level initiatives or the business as a whole.

The challenge for executives and senior leaders is that they delegate the top initiatives to silo parts of their organization and fail to be aligned on clear outcomes, expectations, and the understanding of cross-functional implications. They focus solely on their area of responsibility rather than mentoring their middle managers to understand the entire cross-functional organization, their interdependent relationships, and the business acumen from all department perspectives. Then, they micromanage the decisions and approaches of the Middle Management Team and individual managers when they are no longer close enough to first-level managers and individual contributors to understand the full ramifications of their micro-involvement. This results in confusion and a lack of accountability and ownership from middle managers, and it breaks down confidence and trust in them and their Middle Management Team.

A large multinational chemical manufacturing corporation located in the Middle East purchased a Mexican chemical plant that was previously family-owned. Their directive from Corporate was to increase their operational effectiveness in preparation for growth. Some of the changes they were expected to make included:

FAMILY-OWNED BUSINESS	CORPORATE PARTNER
• Work is accomplished through historic experience based on seniority.	• Create standard operating procedures to improve consistency and to develop new employees.
• Sales are relationship based, favor based, and transactional.	• Sales are based on establishing strategic business partners with clients to improve achievement of customer's strategic goals.
• Human Resources are managed based on long-standing relationships to protect those who don't perform but who are loyal and have relationships outside of the workplace.	• Human Resources are managed based on performance, with consistent practices across the organization eliminating favoritism.

• Professional and leadership development is nonexistent. Leadership practices are top-down and power based.	• Professional and leadership development programs are implemented to improve the development of individuals, engage employees, and implement continuous improvement.
• Leadership is only focused on plant performance and keeping operational practices in a status quo position.	• Leadership is focused on strategic plans for growing the business, developing operational excellence, reducing waste, and contributing to corporate initiatives as a good corporate citizen.

The Senior Leadership Team developed a clear Picture of Success, Team Habits, and Business Priority Projects for being an effective corporate partner. While only seven of the twelve people on the Senior Leadership Team were actively engaged in creating their new team direction, there was no waiting for everyone to "buy in" to their vision.

As the team took action to complete their project commitments and improve their Team Habits, they were able to easily track progress on their projects and improved teamwork within just three months. As a result, three more executives got on board with the commitment of the new Picture of Success, making it a total of ten of the twelve original team members.

By the end of eight months, the plant transformed their organization by accomplishing their project outcomes and by improving teamwork for the Senior Leadership and Middle Management Teams. They won two corporate awards for achieving the greatest level of cost reductions and cross-functional process improvement and implemented a new IT initiative that was now being adopted throughout the corporation. In addition, they established standard operating procedures that raised consistent practices across the plant while implementing a leadership development program to improve supervisory skills and employee engagement.

The two senior leaders who fought against the progress of the plant were provided retirement packages to leave the organization and replaced by new senior leaders over time who were advocates for the Team's Picture of Success.

TRANSFORMING DEPARTMENTS INTO HIGH-PERFORMING TEAMS

There are key departments that either accelerate or hinder organizational success, depending on their level of cooperation and commitment to organizational outcomes. Some of these key departments include Information Systems, Human Resources, and Purchasing. As central departments, they can either support the line organization in making effective decisions and timely implementation or be a roadblock to smooth operations with overcomplicated bureaucracy, over-controlling posturing, and not understanding the business challenges and needs of the line organization.

This was the case for the Human Resources (HR) Department of a manufacturing plant. Instead of being perceived as a support to the plant, they were viewed as a hinderance to getting things done. They spent more time policing HR policies and procedures instead of being problem solvers to accelerate the line departments in responding to customers, growing their managers and employees, and streamlining the ability of the business units in hiring and onboarding new promising employees while promptly and effectively letting go of employees who weren't fitting into the organization. Many times, the different technical areas within HR weren't talking with each other, and the rest of the organization was confused about who to contact to get questions answered.

The HR Department Management Team had to change their mindset from one of power and control to one of partnership with the business unit leaders. Instead of being perfection-oriented, they needed to be more effective problem solvers and streamline processes and approaches for greater speed and responsiveness. Finally, they needed to develop a better understanding of the business so that they could anticipate their needs and challenges to provide more effective strategies for supporting business growth and customer support.

The HR Department Management Team created their Picture of Success for operating as business partners, agreed on Team Habits to work more effectively and collaboratively, and identified projects to improve their responsiveness to their business unit partners. Unfortunately, they allowed themselves to get too bogged down in day-to-day crises, continuing to police the organization and ignoring their team commitments.

When I returned to the team to evaluate their effectiveness, they reported very few accomplishments. They had improved only 25% of their Team Habits instead of the expected 60%, and had improved only 2% in Team Relationships instead of the standard 15% average improvement. These dramatically low scores are very rare, and the reason is always the same: the teams never followed their own processes and didn't keep their commitments—a complete breakdown in accountability with lots of excuses to stay in denial rather than owning the breakdown.

This team was no different. They started off by blaming the team process: "It's too complicated, there are too many commitments, we don't have enough time to implement, and our VP of HR (Senior Management Team leader) isn't effective enough." Knowing that the HR Management Team needed to make a clear commitment to do things differently, I asked them to meet by themselves while I stepped out of the room. I told them there was no point in me wasting my time or theirs if they weren't going to commit to the process and that they should decide among themselves whether or not they wanted to continue. It took forty-five minutes for them to discuss, decide on, and develop a new commitment. When I returned to the team, they not only shared their commitment but also told me how they were planning to change their meetings and priorities and commit to their original agreements from our initial session. I let them know that they only had a month to demonstrate actions on their new commitment, and I would be evaluating them as a team three months later.

Sometimes a wake-up call and a sense of urgency can be the biggest motivator for change, so I never view this situation as negative—just what the team needed to propel them forward.

Three months later when I returned to the team, they were acting like a completely different group. They had stronger team spirit, demonstrated a much higher level of accountability to their commitments, and were more direct in their communications within the team.

They made several accomplishments, received a customer service award from the business units, and improved 75% of their Team Habits. They also had a 25% overall average improvement in their Team Relationships. While it ended up taking them a total of nine months instead of six to make the transformation, they achieved a huge amount of change and saved the VP of HR's job as the leader of the team.

ACCELERATING PROJECT TEAM EXECUTION AND SUCCESS

Project teams have sophisticated planning tools that lay out the steps for different functional areas involved in a project. Methods such as Miro, Microsoft Project, and Prosci are excellent for planning projects, clarifying roles, and identifying the interconnections among different functional responsibilities. However, these tools do not address the need for improving Collective Execution of the plans generated. They are great at describing WHAT needs to be accomplished by WHEN but fail to address the HOW of performance execution.

As a result, decisions get made that don't consider unintended consequences, hand-offs get missed between functional areas, changes get made without fully understanding the implications to schedule, quality, and project performance, and meetings review project status but rarely address the cross-functional changes and breakdowns that need additional problem solving.

If teams want to accomplish a big project, they must develop a Picture of Success for optimally achieving the project, create Team Habits for Collective Execution that will help diverse functional areas quickly and effectively make decisions and resolve problems related to the project, and create the necessary Proactive Recovery Plans beyond risk management for technical breakdown that is already a part of effective project planning.

Team meetings must be more focused on proactively surfacing and resolving any obstacles or challenges that might cause a negative impact on schedule or quality in order to get ahead of the problems, prevent crisis management, and effectively account for the ripple effect of problems in one part of the project that affect other areas.

Project teams typically stay together for the shortest period of time compared to other teams. Yet, the standard improvements in Team Habits of 60% to 80% and improved average Team Relationships improvements of 15% to 35% have a significant impact on project performance. As a result, project teams spend less time in crisis and misunderstandings and more time removing obstacles that cause delays. Thus, projects exceed expectations for on-time delivery and quality of results.

SUPPORTING SELF-DIRECTED AND AGILE TEAMS IN RAPID FORMING TO PERFORMING

Self-directed teams generally take place among employees who are directly serving customers and represent the best understanding for improving processes and customer service. Employees are excited about being given a voice and being able to solve the problems and challenges they live with each day. But they can come in with very strong personalities and ideas for solutions that can result in disagreement and conflict. This not only slows down their progress but can result in discouragement, frustration, or even disengagement by some of the team members.

In Amsterdam, they have implemented an amazingly effective home healthcare system that they call "nursing districts." This is where a team of between eight and twelve nurses serve on a self-directed team that leads their service to their particular community within Amsterdam. This organizational structure is so lean that there are only sixteen corporate managers for 600 employees, and this includes all corporate functions, including the CEO, Administration, HR, IT, Finance, Legal, and two coaches for all sixty teams. Each self-directed team not only manages their schedule but also oversees quality, patient satisfaction, financial management, training and development, and patient education.

The CEO shared with me that after three years of implementation and a well-defined onboarding and team-building process with two internal coaches, they didn't have an effective way to quickly get teams up and running. Some teams had informal leaders who were too controlling and not facilitating input from the entire group, while other teams formed cliques early on that created polarization in the team. Additionally, there were some teams that just couldn't deliver on expectations effectively— they were dedicated to patient care but not ensuring that the organizational requirements were being carried out.

After discussing our approach of focusing on a Picture of Success, Team Habits, and Team Outcomes, the CEO implemented the process within his organization for the "broken" teams and new teams starting out. A year after implementation, he shared with me that the Forming, Norming, and Performing stages of team development that used to take two years or more to get through now took only six months with this new process.

GETTING READY TO TAKE YOUR TEAMS TO THEIR NEXT LEVEL OF HIGH PERFORMANCE

Regardless of which teams you want to see achieve breakthrough results, there are key questions to answer to set them up for success. As you can see, the steps are a cyclical process that repeats each year to keep up with how the team has evolved since the last time the assessment was completed.

Part 1: History	Part 2: Direction	Part 3: Execution	Part 4: Follow-Up
1. What are the historic obstacles that the team has experienced in achieving their goals and needs for change?	1. What are the key external drivers that are the impetus for change?	1. How will roles, expectations, leadership, and communication need to expand for all team members?	1. How will the team track progress differently to ensure action, and results?
2. How will future opportunities and challenges for the organization impact your team?	2. How will the organization's business strategy for the next few years drive team changes in how it needs to function?	2. How will inclusion and engagement need to expand to achieve team goals?	2. How will team members support each other through challenges, and difficulties?
3. How will the makeup of the team evolve and change over time and how will that need to be addressed?	3. How will the team's mindset, behaviors, actions, and reactions to challenges & change need to adjust to support organizational priorities?	3. How will teamwork with other teams need to improve for effective cross-functional performance?	3. How will the team establish a habit of non-judgmental learning and continuous improvement?
4. What processes and approaches to achieving goals may not be effective enough in the future to keep up with a changing marketplace?	4. What changes in the team's makeup will take place due to retirement, growth, or restructuring?	4. What will leaders and team members need to "let go of" to create the space for change?	4. How will team members acknowledge, recognize, and celebrate progress as they achieve success?

Figure 12 Assessment to Drive Transformation

A DELIBERATE ROAD MAP

There is nothing more satisfying and gratifying than to experience a well-run team that has high regard and support for each other, demonstrates trust and openness, and accomplishes breakthrough results at the same time. It's fun to be part of this kind of team and know that it isn't luck or time that created a stellar experience, but a deliberate road map that can be measured, repeated, and evolved over time.

Predictability is one of the core competencies of leadership and teams in the future. Dependability, consistency, humor, dedication, due diligence, and human compassion are all attributes of the highest-performing and most sustainable teams. Ultimately, these teams attract and retain the highest performers, develop future leaders, and get the best results.

One of the greatest feelings in life is that of being part of an awesome team—the camaraderie, the trust, the support, the growth, and the accomplishment you feel that brings a smile to your face. Whether it's in sports, music, or business, the experience of being on a great team is exhilarating, fun, and memorable. Now that you know how high-functioning teams operate and what makes a team great, you can recreate that experience with any team you are a part of.

> If you haven't already, check out bstate.com/rt-resources to watch videos regarding Collective Execution, Cross-Functional Teams, and Change Management. And don't forget that you can take my exclusive assessment on that page as well.

Printed in the USA
CPSIA information can be obtained
at www.ICGtesting.com
LVHW011448280823
756520LV00005B/126